D1579662

A GIRL'S GUIDE TO BEING AWESOME

A GIRL'S GUIDE TO BEING AWESOME

Copyright © Suzanne Virdee 2020

Based on *A Teenage Girl's Guide to Being Fabulous!* published in 2015

All rights reserved.

No part of this book may be reproduced by any means, nor transmitted, nor translated into a machine language, without the written permission of the publishers.

Suzanne Virdee has asserted her right to be identified as the author of this work in accordance with sections 77 and 78 of the Copyright, Designs and Patents Act 1988.

Condition of Sale
This book is sold subject to the condition that it shall not, by way of trade or otherwise, be lent, resold, hired out or otherwise circulated in any form of binding or cover other than that in which it is published and without a similar condition including this condition being imposed on the subsequent purchaser.

An Hachette UK Company
www.hachette.co.uk

Vie Books, an imprint of Summersdale Publishers Ltd
Part of Octopus Publishing Group Limited
Carmelite House
50 Victoria Embankment
LONDON
EC4Y 0DZ
UK

www.summersdale.com

Printed and bound in the Czech Republic

ISBN: 978-1-78783-536-8

Substantial discounts on bulk quantities of Summersdale books are available to corporations, professional associations and other organizations. For details contact general enquiries: telephone: +44 (0) 1243 771107 or email: enquiries@summersdale.com.

The author and the publisher cannot accept responsibility for any misuse or misunderstanding of any information contained herein, or any loss, damage or injury, be it health, financial or otherwise, suffered by any individual or group acting upon or relying on information contained herein. None of the views or suggestions in this book is intended to replace medical opinion from a doctor. If you have concerns about your physical or mental health, please seek professional advice.

To Isla

From G.U. Am
Pilan

A GIRL'S GUIDE TO BEING AWESOME

EMPOWERING
ADVICE FOR
TEENAGE LIFE

SUZANNE VIRDEE

Xmas . 2022

vie

TO ISLA

FROM G. V. JIM

xx

This book is dedicated to every girl, everywhere.
For those who already have dreams and want to
make them come true, and for those who don't yet
dare to dream. I hope this book empowers you.

It is also dedicated to my beautiful mother, Cynthia,
whose love, wisdom and never-ending support has
enabled me to believe in myself, and has given me
the power to follow and achieve my dreams.

Finally, this book is dedicated to my dad,
Mohan, whose advice to "never give up" has
served me well in every part of my life.

XMAS :-) 2022

ABOUT THE AUTHOR

Suzanne Virdee is a journalist. She was ten years old when she decided she wanted to make journalism her career. Growing up, she wrote and produced newspapers for her family, selling them for ten pence each. After finishing her A levels, she decided against advice to go to university and set out to find a career as a reporter instead.

Suzanne spent the summer after she had finished school writing (there was no email then – imagine that!) to around 90 local newspapers and radio newsrooms all over the UK, asking to be taken on as a junior reporter. Instead of a promising offer, the result of all her efforts was a heap of rejection letters.

Feeling down but not defeated, she wrote to the *Solihull Times* newspaper in the West Midlands, offering to work for a week as a volunteer. They decided to take her on and, due to another reporter being off ill, she ended up writing the entertainment news page and getting her first byline.

By the end of the week her fortunes had completely changed. The editor called her into his office, impressed by her work writing the entertainment news, and offered her a job as a trainee reporter. She was on her way then, and she has never looked back.

She went on to work for a daily newspaper in Birmingham called the *Birmingham Evening Mail* before switching to broadcast journalism. She worked for BBC radio and then regional ITV News before being headhunted to present the BBC regional news programme *Midlands Today* – a job that saw her win a Best Presenter award. She also became a regular face on *BBC Breakfast News*.

Suzanne is currently freelance and presents the *ITV National Weekend News* and *ITV News* in London, as well as working for the BBC.

She lives in Worcestershire with her husband Andrew Fox, an award-winning photojournalist.

CONTENTS

A LITTLE BIT ABOUT ME

I'm the daughter of a white English mother and an Indian father. Sadly it was – and is to this day – seen by many families across India as undesirable to have a baby girl. That's the case in many other countries too.

In my dad's country, India, culturally it's boys who are prized above girls. It's the family of the groom that receives dowries from the bride's family before a wedding. Dowries are usually gifts of money, but can also be gifts of jewellery, clothes, or even a car. Although dowries are against the law in India, in reality it's a tradition that's still expected by many. This puts a big financial burden on the bride-to-be's family. You can perhaps understand, then, why having a girl is not always seen as desirable in Indian culture.

Luckily, my dad is among those forward-thinking men who cherish girls just as much as boys. He told me from a young age (as he still does now): "You are both a son and a daughter to me; I love you, and I want the same things for you as I would for a son." Hearing this and having many strong-minded women in my family – my amazing mother being just one of them – helped to make me strong, and better able to cope with the ups and downs that life brings.

It has meant that I have always believed that I am just as good as anybody else – boys included! It also taught me to be fearless and go for what I want in life.

The "can do" mentality I learned from my mum and dad gave me the belief that I could achieve my dream of being a journalist. Even when I was told by careers advisers that this vocation was too difficult to break into, it was my parents' encouragement and their belief in me that spurred me on and gave me such a positive and determined outlook.

As far as I'm concerned, this is the message all parents, teachers – and the rest of society – should give to all girls, no matter what their age.

Sure, it can be pretty hard growing up a girl, but there's nothing you can't achieve if you put your mind to it.

What qualifications do I have for writing this book? Well, I was a girl and now I am a woman. If I hadn't had such positive encouragement from my parents and family, I may never have developed the self-belief and determination that I needed to achieve my dreams.

My extraordinary family, as well as my life experiences, have taught me so much – and these are things that I want you to know too. That is why I have written this book: because I want you to know – whoever you are and wherever you are reading this – that you can achieve anything you set your mind to.

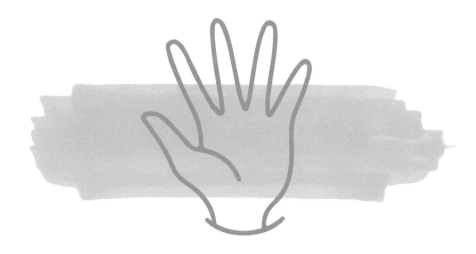

INTRODUCTION

There's no great secret to how to be an awesome girl. It's not just something that's reserved for the rich and beautiful – it's a state of mind, and it's something we can all be. We are all born awesome, but for some of us the feeling can be knocked out of us as we grow up. A harsh word here, or a bad experience there, can leave us feeling anything but awesome.

Another factor that may knock our confidence as we grow up is how quickly we're expected to become adults.

Teenage years are a time of growth and change. It's a time that is both exciting and scary. Schoolwork suddenly gets serious and there's huge pressure to succeed in your exams so that you can get a good job – even when you may not have the faintest clue what job that might be!

How you look becomes more important too. There's pressure from adverts and society generally for your looks to conform to a certain stereotype.

It's also a time when your teenage hormones kick in, and all of a sudden sex and relationships become important and a "hot topic" among you and your friends.

On top of all those pressures, there's the added 24/7 distraction of social media, which, though it allows you to stay in touch with friends and be creative, can take you to some dark places if you let it!

None of this would be so hard to deal with if there were instructions on how to handle teenage life – but there is no rule book. What you do is up to you. And even though choice is a great thing, just how do you use your freedom wisely?

I hope my book will give you food for thought about that. My job here is not to brainwash you to think one thing or another but to spur you on to decide for yourself what sort of world you want to live in, what you want to achieve with your life, and how to make it happen.

Soon you'll realize how awesome it is to be you!

YOU ARE
CAPABLE
OF
AMAZING
THINGS

CHAPTER ONE

FIND YOUR SPARKLE

WHAT IS "SPARKLE"?

Sparkle is an energy; it's a vibrancy around a person. Sparkle is that thing that gets us noticed for all the right reasons. It's inside all of us, but you may not even realize you have it.

Sparkle also means believing in yourself and breaking down barriers so you can get to where you want to be.

"SUCCESSFUL WOMEN HAVE AN AURA THAT SAYS 'I BELONG IN THIS SEAT'."

CATHIE BLACK, MEDIA EXECUTIVE AND AUTHOR

One famous example of a woman who stepped out of the boundaries of expectation and went on to achieve great things is the American senior politician Alexandria Ocasio-Cortez. In 2019, Alexandria was named one of the world's most influential women.

Although she wasn't born into a wealthy or powerful family (her mother came from Puerto Rico and her father from an area of New York called the South Bronx), Alexandria worked her way from being a waitress all the way to being voted into the US Congress.

She achieved something that people with her age and social status don't often do, because she was able to recognize and utilize the sparkle she had inside herself.

"I FELT LIKE THE ONLY WAY TO EFFECTIVELY RUN FOR OFFICE IS IF YOU HAD ACCESS TO A LOT OF WEALTH, HIGH SOCIAL INFLUENCE, A LOT OF DYNASTIC POWER, AND I KNEW THAT I DIDN'T HAVE ANY OF THOSE THINGS."

ALEXANDRIA OCASIO-CORTEZ, US POLITICIAN

Alexandria could see her limitations: she didn't have wealth, or a family with the connections to help her reach her goal. But the things she did have were far more important than all that: Alexandria had self-belief, passion and determination. All these qualities are things that make a person sparkle and stand out from the crowd.

Alexandria believed she had the right to become a congresswoman just as much as those with money and power behind them did. She made history in America by becoming the youngest-ever woman to be elected to the House of Representatives, aged just 29.

Sparkle is about unleashing the natural talent inside you just like Alexandria did. It doesn't mean being "cool" or being the most popular girl at school. It means quietly but firmly believing in yourself, and not allowing anyone to make you feel inferior. It means feeling you belong and feeling you can do anything.

Everyone who's achieved great things in life has sparkle, but they don't have it as a result of what they've achieved – they had it before they hit the big time. They used sparkle to achieve that success. You can too!

Don't get sparkle mixed up with showing off though – it's more than that. Sparkle is genuine and it's what we all need to carry us through the good and not-so-good times.

Those of you reading this book will probably come from all sorts of different backgrounds. Some of you will have more money than others, more opportunities and more support at home than others. Some of you may feel alone or feel you have no one who seems to care about what you do.

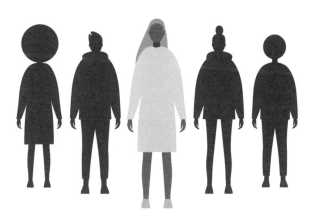

You might have parents who expect you to follow a certain path and profession and who might pile a lot of pressure on you. You may have recently come to this country with your family and be getting used to a whole new culture. Money may be tight and opportunities where you live may be limited. You may not have a mum, or you may not have a dad; in fact, you may not have either. You may be in care or living with another family. Whatever your situation, try not to be too worried or anxious about how things are right now, because **it doesn't matter where you come from – it's where you are going that counts.**

Whatever is happening in your world right now won't stay that way forever. You're growing up, and life will change. It can change for the better or for the worse: that bit is up to you – and that's where the need for sparkle comes in.

Sit and dream for a minute. What career or job do you wish you could have when you leave school or university?

Now, think about what job you really think you'll end up doing when you leave school or university.

If you've answered the same for both questions, that's brilliant! You're on track. However, if the two answers are wildly different, then you haven't unlocked your inner sparkle yet.

What I want you to automatically believe is that your dreams can become reality if you put your mind to it – just like Alexandria did.

No matter what your personal dreams are for your life – whether you want to be a florist or a film director – sparkle will help you get there.

MY GOALS AND AMBITIONS

Use this page to note down some of your goals, dreams and ambitions. Your sparkle will help you to achieve them!

_____

_____

_____

_____

_____

_____

_____

_____

_____

_____

_____

_____

_____

_____

_____

_____

_____

_____

_____

SPARKLE AT SCHOOL

Going to school is very different to being in the adult world of work. You can get by at school without drawing attention to yourself. But if you're going to succeed in the big wide world, you need to make yourself stand out. You need sparkle.

Employers often tell me that they hate it when candidates in interviews mumble, don't hold eye contact, and just generally have no personality. Sparkle gives you the confidence to communicate well, and that's a big key to success. Good communication allows you to get your message across clearly and gives people confidence in you.

So, how do you – as a young woman – go about getting sparkle, if even the thought of speaking in public, or to a teacher, fills you with dread?

"I ALWAYS DID SOMETHING I WAS A LITTLE NOT READY TO DO.
I THINK THAT'S HOW YOU GROW. WHEN THERE'S THAT MOMENT OF
'WOW, I'M NOT REALLY SURE I CAN DO THIS', AND YOU PUSH THROUGH
THOSE MOMENTS, THAT'S WHEN YOU HAVE A BREAKTHROUGH."

MARISSA MAYER, GOOGLE'S FIRST FEMALE ENGINEER AND FORMER BOSS AT YAHOO

That's pretty much how you do it – you push through the fear.

For generations, girls have been "the quiet ones". Often, when girls want to say something, they don't say it out of fear they'll be laughed at. How many times have you not put your hand up at school when you knew the answer to a teacher's question, for fear your classmates will all turn to look at you if you're wrong – even when you know you're right?

When we feel like that, we are letting fear hold us back.

So, how do we boot fear out and bring the sparkle in? First of all, prepare, prepare, prepare – preparation is the key to everything. When you prepare, you feel confident; when you feel confident, you sparkle.

Let's work through this: before you have an important conversation – say, with an adult – stop and think through exactly what you want to say and practise it. Hear yourself speaking the words, make sure you're speaking clearly and not too quietly and that you're holding eye contact. Think of the best outcome that could happen from your conversation, and the worst.

For example, if you're asking permission from a teacher to audition for the school play, the best outcome would be that they say "yes", and if they do: that's great; job done! The worst outcome would be that they say "no", and you might feel really disappointed. So, do you just accept it and walk away feeling sad, or do you have a persuasive and good reason up your sleeve as to why they should give you a go?

I hope you're feeling the sparkle now and thinking that you would be someone to persuade your teacher. The next step then is to ask why they're not giving you a try and then give them a great reason why they should. You may change their mind! And even if you don't, you'll look keen and confident, and you'll leave them with the impression that you don't give up easily. If you can't get your words out then you may lose the chance of doing what you wanted, as well as the chance to make a good impression. That's what I mean by preparing for different outcomes.

Let's look at another example of using sparkle to push through the fear: imagine you have to talk to the class, host an assembly, or take part in a debate at school. If that's making you feel a bit queasy, bear with me. Let's practise this.

Take a couple of long, slow deep breaths; really breathe in through your nose and out through your mouth. Now, close your eyes and imagine yourself in that very situation. See every detail of you being called up to walk on to the stage or to the front of the class. Feel every step of the way, see all the people around you looking at you and let yourself feel how terrifying that could be. Let yourself feel the nerves. Then see yourself getting to the stage or the front of the class and looking at all the faces waiting for you to speak – eek! Think how it'll feel when you get there and you have to start speaking.

I'm aware this might sound a bit crazy but visualizing every step of a "scary" scenario can really help take the fear out of a situation. Once you've got used to how it will look and feel to do something in your head, doing it for real won't feel anywhere near as terrifying.

So, now you're up there ready to speak. Before you do, take a deep breath in and out, smile at your audience and try not to rush what you're saying. If you're doing a speech or presentation, print it out. Typed words are easier to read than handwriting, and you're less likely to stumble or lose your way.

Before you read it for real to your audience, practise saying it all out loud – over and over again – so you're used to the sound of your voice and know what you're saying. That way you don't have to stare down at your notes all the time. Look up and connect with your audience now and then. There will be a big temptation for you to get through the ordeal as quickly as you can. Many people make the mistake of talking far too fast, and it's really hard then for your audience to understand what you're saying. So, ensure you make an extra effort to speak slowly and clearly.

These tips really do work, and when you've nailed them, you've nailed the nerves – then you'll realize you do have sparkle.

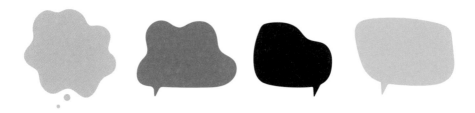

If speaking in front of lots of people still terrifies you, just think of them all on the toilet... or naked! Grim, but it will make you laugh, and laughing will relax you. Remember they're only human like you, no matter how important they are!

Speaking in public terrifies so many adults, so if you can learn to do it well and keep the nerves at bay now, you'll not only stand out, but you'll have learned a valuable communication tool that will help you through your whole life.

Nerves and shyness are a waste of time and really hold us back. If you prepare well, practise and stay focused, the nerves won't get to you as much. You'll be too busy concentrating on what you're doing or saying.

In my job as a TV news presenter, I have to do a lot of interviews with all sorts of well-known and famous people – from Hollywood actors to senior politicians – as well as reading the news to millions of people. If I got nervous, I'd fall apart and wouldn't be able to do my job. Staying focused on what you're doing is key.

Trust me, these tips do work, and the more you use them the easier it gets. You'll soon find the sparkle. You'll also find that your classmates and teachers and other adults will be blown away by your confidence. Someone who looks and sounds confident always stands out for the right reasons.

Fear holds you back in life, sparkle pushes you forward, and practice makes perfect.

People who achieve their dreams often say they didn't have any doubts or fear about what they were doing. In other words, they just concentrated on the end result and those horrible nagging doubts didn't have time to get inside their heads and wreck their plans. *This* is what sparkle is.

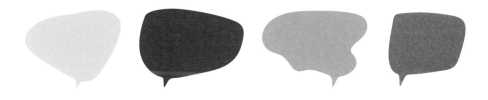

DON'T LET ANYONE DULL YOUR SPARKLE

SPARKLE IN THE BIG WIDE WORLD

For many of you reading this, your life will more than likely consist of being at home and being at school. You may feel distinctly "unsparkly" right now! But what I want to encourage you to do is to step outside your comfort zone and into the big wide world.

Learning new things makes us more confident and it helps shape our personality. So, if you can, get a part-time job, join an after-school club, or volunteer somewhere. Open your eyes and experience new things.

If you already do some out-of-school activities, that's great. Think about what you're getting out of them. Are you enjoying them? Are you meeting new people? Are you learning new things? If the answer is no to any of these questions, change what you're doing and try something new.

By trying lots of new things, you might find that you're really good at something you never even thought of doing – it might even open up a whole new career path!

"I FELT LIKE IT WAS TIME TO SET UP MY FUTURE, SO I SET A GOAL. MY GOAL WAS INDEPENDENCE."

BEYONCÉ, AMERICAN SINGER-SONGWRITER

Beyoncé has nailed sparkle and achieved her goal of independence. Your future is yours to shape too. Just set your goal – whatever it is – and work toward it. No one else can make your dreams come true for you. Though others might be able to help you, achieving your goals is down to you.

Having your voice heard as a teenage girl is important, as it brings confidence (which in turn brings sparkle!). Unfortunately, this doesn't always happen – especially when girls are still at school. As young as you are now, you should be able to speak up and have a platform for discussing the things that matter to you.

Perhaps you could start an online school newspaper or, if your school has the facilities, a radio station. All you need is a few like-minded pupils to join you (and, of course, your head teacher's permission!). If you're given the go-ahead, your teachers can help you with your project.

Doing something like this is a great confidence boost not just for you, but all the other girls around you too. This kind of thing can help girls to come together and feel empowered and listened to. On a practical level, it also gives you a platform to help get the things you think are unfair changed. When the boys see what you're achieving they'll soon be clamouring to get involved too!

Maybe you could start a "Girls' Club" at your school? Ask teachers for advice and guidance on how to go about this. It's a great opportunity to get to know people but also discuss the more serious issues girls face, such as loneliness, the pressure to be and act a certain way, stress around social media and schoolwork.

Use your girls' group to inspire you too. Invite successful women – maybe a sportswoman, a doctor, a pilot or an actor – to come and talk to you about their career and how they got to where they are. Hearing their stories will really motivate you.

Talking openly to other people and sharing experiences can make you feel so much better about yourself. You will soon realize that what worries you also worries them. You can support and find strength in one another, and that's a really positive thing.

Doing things outside the school curriculum sets you apart from the crowd. It'll also look awesome on your CV and will be a great talking point when you go for interviews. It might seem a bit early to be thinking about this, but trust me, interviewers are often looking for candidates who are different and have something special to offer.

MY EXTRACURRICULAR ACTIVITIES

Use this page to note down some of the things you would like to work on outside of your studies.

BELIEVE YOU CAN

As I've mentioned, sparkle is all about believing in yourself.

The Swedish schoolgirl and environmental activist Greta Thunberg is a great example of this. In 2018, when Greta decided to speak up about climate change, she was just 15 years old; she has since attracted lots of criticism because she's so outspoken and is not afraid to voice her opinions. Greta is a hero to some and an annoyance to others, but she doesn't let the haters stop her.

Greta bravely stands up for what she believes in and, as young as she is, she carries on despite the nasty things said about her on social media; her personal strength is amazing. She isn't afraid to discuss the issues she's passionate about in front of some of the most powerful world leaders.

Greta teaches us not just about issues around climate change, but a lot about what a young woman can achieve if she believes in herself. Her speech at the United Nations Climate Action Summit in 2019 got well over three million views online – no posing or pouting needed!

Unfortunately, in spite of the amazing work Greta does in raising awareness around climate change, some have chosen to criticize her for the way she looks.

> "WHEN HATERS GO AFTER YOUR LOOKS AND DIFFERENCES [SHE HAS ASPERGER SYNDROME], IT MEANS THEY HAVE NOWHERE LEFT TO GO. AND THEN YOU KNOW YOU'RE WINNING!"
>
> GRETA THUNBERG, SWEDISH ENVIRONMENTAL ACTIVIST

Although she's right, these comments likely still hurt Greta – but it's her sparkle that makes her resilient to the name-calling. Perhaps Greta would agree with the following words, from a woman who lived many years before her:

> "YOU GAIN STRENGTH, COURAGE AND CONFIDENCE BY EVERY
> EXPERIENCE IN WHICH YOU REALLY STOP TO LOOK FEAR IN THE FACE...
> YOU MUST DO THE THING YOU THINK YOU CANNOT DO."

ELEANOR ROOSEVELT, US FIRST LADY, DIPLOMAT AND HUMAN RIGHTS ACTIVIST

Greta is proof that these words are true. It must have been daunting and scary to face all the world leaders who were at the UN Climate Action Summit, but she still did it, and she didn't run away from saying what she wanted to.

A friend of mine who runs confidence workshops told me that when she asked a group of teenage girls to each tell her one thing they thought was good about themselves, or that they were good at, no one put their hand up. She left it as long as she could – thinking they were shy – before asking them again. Then came the surprising and depressing answer from one girl, who blurted out: "I'm not good at anything".

It turned out that many of the girls in the group had never been told they were good at anything. In fact, some had been told the opposite: that they were useless and were never going to make anything of themselves. Sadly, the girls actually believed that this was true.

This meant the girls had given up on having dreams for their future, even though their lives had barely begun. Their sparkle was extinguished by the unkind words of others. Don't let that happen to you. You have to believe you are just as good as anyone else – because you are!

> "SOME PEOPLE SAY I HAVE ATTITUDE – MAYBE I DO. BUT I THINK
> THAT YOU HAVE TO. YOU HAVE TO BELIEVE IN YOURSELF WHEN NO
> ONE ELSE DOES – THAT MAKES YOU A WINNER RIGHT THERE."

VENUS WILLIAMS, US PROFESSIONAL TENNIS PLAYER

If you don't have this sort of belief in yourself and your abilities, then it's unlikely that you'll succeed. It doesn't matter if ten other people all think you can do something – if you don't believe it, you won't achieve it.

MAKE HERSTORY

Sometimes it can seem like boys have more of a "can do" attitude than girls. Perhaps this is understandable when you think about the roles of men and women throughout history.

Traditionally it was the men who would go out to work and the women who would stay at home. Men saw themselves (and were seen by society) as breadwinners. Even when women started to go out to work, they would often work part-time, so it was always the man's career that was seen as most important.

Sadly, while this is no longer the way most countries operate, the general attitude is still so deeply ingrained in most societies that even now it can be a novelty to hear about female breadwinners and men who stay at home. It's still a novelty to see female world leaders, successful female scientists or multimillionaire businesswomen.

When we do hear about these women, we also often hear about their looks or even how their children might be suffering if they are working long hours! Yet hardly anyone will question who is looking after a man's children when he works. These are the sexist criticisms that, without us realizing, we've grown used to. These beliefs can make us less likely to believe in ourselves and to succeed.

> "IT'S REALLY IMPORTANT THAT YOUNG WOMEN BE REMINDED THAT THEIR INVOLVEMENT MATTERS AND THAT THEIR VOICE IS HEARD. EVEN IF IT FEELS LIKE IT'S SMALL, IT REALLY CAN MAKE AN IMPACT."
>
> ### MEGHAN MARKLE, DUCHESS OF SUSSEX AND ACTOR

A woman who is passionate and assertive is often described as "a bitch" or "bossy". These are both negative, insulting words. When a man is assertive, he is more likely to be seen as "strong" or "decisive", which are complimentary and positive words. These are the double standards that exist between successful men and successful women. While it's important to be aware of this sexism, it's also important to have enough self-belief and sparkle to not let it hold you back.

One woman who is sure to inspire you is space scientist Dr Maggie Aderin-Pocock. She has dealt with people doubting her abilities all her life.

"I WAS PUT IN REMEDIAL CLASS AND PEOPLE ASSUMED I WAS NOT GOING TO ACHIEVE VERY MUCH. I DID FEEL WRITTEN OFF... WHEN I GOT MY FIRST JOB WITH THE MINISTRY OF DEFENCE THERE WERE A FEW TIMES I WALKED INTO A ROOM AND SOMEONE WOULD SAY, 'THREE COFFEES, LOVE'... THERE'S THE INITIAL SHOCK BECAUSE PEOPLE AREN'T USED TO SEEING BLACK FEMALE SCIENTISTS OR ENGINEERS."

DR MAGGIE ADERIN-POCOCK, SPACE SCIENTIST AND TV PRESENTER

Maggie's incredible story proves that just because others doubt you or put you down, it doesn't mean they're right – or that you have to take any notice of them!

Maggie experienced the lazy, in-built sexism that we have discussed. Still, she didn't let any silly comments and assumptions dull her sparkle, and neither should you.

Society still has lower expectations for women in the workplace than for men. Often, men achieve more because they believe they can achieve it, and some men believe that success or a promotion is their right. What I would like you to remember is that it is your right as much as it is theirs.

"WE NEED TO RESHAPE OUR OWN PERCEPTION OF HOW WE VIEW OURSELVES."

BEYONCÉ

Don't weigh yourself down with thoughts of all the obstacles that might come your way – instead enjoy the journey of working toward what you want. Take inspiration from other women, because even if they're not doing a job you want to do, they will still be able to teach you some valuable life lessons.

"A GREAT TENNIS CAREER IS SOMETHING THAT A 15-YEAR-OLD NORMALLY DOESN'T HAVE. I HOPE MY EXAMPLE HELPS OTHER TEENS BELIEVE THEY CAN ACCOMPLISH THINGS THEY NEVER THOUGHT POSSIBLE."

MARIA SHARAPOVA, RUSSIAN FORMER PROFESSIONAL TENNIS PLAYER

There are amazing women out there of all ages and from all kinds of backgrounds doing amazing things – and you can too! Don't be afraid to sparkle and you'll shine bright in whatever you choose to do.

HOW AM I GOING TO USE MY SPARKLE?

Now that you know all about the sparkle inside of you, use this page to note down some of the things that you want to use it for.

YOU
ONLY
FAIL
WHEN
YOU
STOP
TRYING

CHAPTER TWO
FAB-U-CATION

OK, I completely made this word up, but "fab-u-cation" is the word that reminds us what education can do – it makes us fab!

"I NEVER CUT CLASS. I LOVED GETTING 'A'S. I LIKED BEING SMART. I LIKED BEING ON TIME. I THOUGHT BEING SMART IS COOLER THAN ANYTHING IN THE WORLD."

MICHELLE OBAMA, FORMER FIRST LADY OF THE US, LAWYER AND AUTHOR

As Michelle Obama says: being smart is cooler than anything in the world. And, girls, the great news is you are smart – actually, you are really smart. Statistically, girls tend to do better than boys at school – even in countries where women lack equal rights with men.

Despite this, girls are more likely to doubt their intelligence. Yes, even though you're a very bright spark, you probably don't believe it about yourself. Study after study has found that you probably wouldn't describe yourself as intelligent or clever, whereas boys are likely to do so.

So why don't you believe it? Well, maybe it's because we're perfectionists, or maybe it's because we see men as natural leaders in life because of the stereotypes we've grown up with. Whatever the reason, thinking like this can hold you back – you must break out of this mindset.

Across the world there are more women than men going to university. Unfortunately, though, girls are still a minority in the STEM subjects (science, technology, engineering and maths). These areas are where the big earning potential is, but a study in 2018 showed girls are often put off because they feel the courses are "male dominated or difficult".* By not choosing these subjects, you're removing yourself from some of the highest-earning jobs out there – jobs that many of you reading this have the ability to do.

* Institute for Fiscal Studies, "Why Don't More Girls Study Maths and Physics?" (2018)

I'm certainly not telling you what you should study and what job you should have – that's up to you – just that you should never limit yourself.

FALL IN LOVE WITH LEARNING

As soon as we're born, we start learning. As we grow, we become increasingly curious and we want to know about everything around us. Do you remember picking up things when you were little and putting them in your mouth? That was you trying to find out what it was, what it was for and how to use it. We're born inquisitive. Toys taught us colours and shapes, and we excitedly leafed through books we couldn't even read yet, desperate to know what they were all about. Learning at that time was exciting and joyful.

Staying excited and joyful about learning is the key. Although girls tend to do well at school, they are often tough on themselves. Girls tend to be more disciplined than boys and serious about their work. They also often worry more about getting the right grades, which can cause them a lot of stress.

If you've been studying really hard for a test and you don't get full marks, are you gutted? Do you feel you've let yourself down? If you do (though it's certainly not an uncommon feeling), you are putting far too much pressure on yourself. While aiming to be the best is admirable, it's not good if it makes you feel ill.

So, here are some tips on how you can start to make your schoolwork a bit less stressful:

ONE

DON'T BE TOO HARD ON YOURSELF: be pleased when you do well and if you didn't get the score you wanted, don't beat yourself up. Talk to the teacher to find out where you went wrong and what you can do to improve next time.

TWO

DO HOMEWORK WITH A FRIEND: when you're with someone who also wants to do well, you'll naturally encourage one another, and learning will seem easier. It's also more fun! You can test each other too – so you get an idea of whether what you're learning is going in!

THREE

TAKE BREAKS: get outside, walk the dog (if you have one) or dance to your music. Do whatever it is that will turn your brain off "study mode" and let it relax for a while. Your brain can only take in so much information at one time – it needs regular time out.

These tips are pretty much the same as when you're studying for big exams, but then you may also want to:

ONE

MAKE A REVISION TIMETABLE: list the areas that are your weakest and set aside more time to work through them.

TWO

ASK IF YOU NEED HELP: if there's something you don't understand, ask for an explanation. If you carry on blindly, trying to learn something you don't really get, it won't go in. I can assure you your teachers will be thrilled to be asked.

THREE

WORK OUT WHERE YOU WORK BEST: once you work out where you study best, you can do your work there. It may not be your quiet bedroom where your stuff is all around you and you can get easily distracted, but perhaps a library or at school.

WORKING AT MY BEST

Use this page to note down some of the tips that you think would work best for you, as well as any other ideas you can think of to improve your studying.

_____

_____

_____

_____

_____

_____

_____

_____

_____

_____

_____

_____

_____

_____

_____

_____

_____

_____

_____

_____

_____

_____

_____

_____

_____

WHAT'S THE POINT?

When we're at school there're a whole range of lessons on our timetable. While it's easy to dismiss many of them as "boring" or "pointless", because we can't see how they'll help us in life, the fact is that the wide range of subjects we're exposed to in school allows us to work out what we're good at and what we enjoy. No subject should be dismissed.

I remember moaning to my friends at school about this very feeling. I used to say: "What's the point of doing woodwork – I'm never going to be a carpenter!" Now I understand that even though I have never wanted to be a carpenter, those lessons were a good insight into something I would never have had the opportunity to do (or been bothered to try) otherwise. Plus, even though I moaned, I still have the chopping board I made in school – and I'm very proud of it!

Doing woodwork also taught me how to use a big saw, which came in very handy when I had to saw the bottom off one of my doors at home that was sticking!

My point is, there's a purpose to everything. Learning different things expands our minds.

What's even more amazing is that a subject you thought of as a hobby – such as cooking, music, art or sport – may end up being a career for you. The so-called "serious subjects" are all well and good (and need our attention), but other subjects can help us to work out where our talents lie too. Some subjects also use different parts of our brain and let us switch off from the "heavy" subjects, like maths or science. Some of us aren't suited to academia and some people might be artistic and better at doing creative things. School is your chance to find out what your talents are, so you can develop them if you want to.

Education, no matter what subject we're taught – or whether we're going to make it our career or not – widens our knowledge base, and that makes us more interesting people. Having a large knowledge base also makes it more likely that we'll be able to make good conversation with a wide range of people – this is a useful tool in life. If you can see school as a timetable of experiences, rather than a list of "useful" and "useless" subjects, it'll make it more enjoyable.

"EDUCATION IS THE KEY TO UNLOCKING THE WORLD, A PASSPORT TO FREEDOM."

OPRAH WINFREY, AMERICAN TALK-SHOW HOST, ACTOR AND PHILANTHROPIST

BE YOUR OWN PERSON

Many of us want to get a good job or have a good career when we leave education. I don't think the majority of you reading this would say the opposite – after all, it gives us a purpose, financial freedom and allows us to be independent. But when you're young, there are lots of distractions. It's not always easy to be motivated to do schoolwork; sometimes it seems boring, or classmates can be disruptive and distracting. Perhaps your friends encourage you to bunk off, leaving you behind with lessons, or your own family thinks it's a waste of time. You may look around where you live and see the job prospects are bleak – there may not be much money in the jobs available there and it may seem to you that you have no way out. The thing is: education is your way out.

"ONE CHILD, ONE TEACHER, ONE BOOK, ONE PEN CAN CHANGE THE WORLD."

MALALA YOUSAFZAI, PAKISTANI ACTIVIST FOR FEMALE EDUCATION
AND THE YOUNGEST-EVER NOBEL PRIZE LAUREATE

Maybe no one in your family has passed an exam but this fact doesn't mean that you can't pass an exam either, because you can. No matter what your circumstances, education is always worthwhile, and what you do with it when you're grown up is up to you. Your education will always be valuable.

STRIVE

FOR

PROGRESS,

NOT

PERFECTION

Whoever your family are, and what they have – or have not – achieved in their lives, shouldn't impact what you achieve. Just because the adults in your life might be accountants, that doesn't mean you have to be one too. Or just because your mum and dad don't work, that doesn't mean you shouldn't either.

Even though you're still young, now is a great time to start thinking about what job you would like to have when you grow up. There are thousands of different jobs out there; some careers exist that you wouldn't even think were careers. Have you ever thought about becoming an astronaut, a chocolatier, a translator, musician, politician, a make-up artist for TV or film actors, a hotel manager, a fashion designer, a coder, a clothes buyer for an exclusive store like Selfridges or even a store like Bloomingdale's in New York? Do any of these jobs sound too good to be true? Well, they're not! If a job exists in this world, there is no reason why you can't do it.

> "MY BROTHER, DAVID, WAS EIGHTEEN MONTHS OLDER SO ANYTHING HE COULD DO, I WANTED TO DO – AND THERE WAS NEVER ANY DIFFERENTIATION BETWEEN US. MY PARENTS NEVER SAID: 'DAVID CAN GO RACING AND YOU CAN STAY AT HOME AND PLAY WITH BARBIE'."

> SUSIE WOLFF, SCOTTISH FORMER RACING DRIVER

When I said I wanted to be a journalist, I was persuaded to think again by my college principal, who said: "It's a very difficult career to get into." While that was true, I knew that I wanted to do it, and I wasn't going to let one person's opinion – or the fact it wasn't a particularly easy career to get into – put me off. I knew it was right for me and that I would be good at it. I was prepared to ignore the "advice" I was given and plough on to achieve my dream – you should feel ready to do the same.

> **"I THINK YOU CAN HAVE IT ALL. YOU JUST HAVE TO WORK REALLY HARD, BECAUSE GREAT THINGS DON'T COME EASILY."**
>
> **KATY PERRY, AMERICAN SINGER-SONGWRITER**

When you know what you want to do, it makes school and schoolwork much more relevant. You should feel fired up and excited, realizing that school is just a stepping stone to bigger things.

I've not met anyone who messed about at school and left with no qualifications who wouldn't seize the opportunity to go back and do it again. Find your purpose, and even if you don't know yet what you want to do for a job, just take each lesson for what it is: a chance to gain knowledge, and a window on to different worlds.

Millions of girls across the world are prevented from getting an education, and many of them would love to go to school and have the opportunities in life that you do. When you're finding it difficult to motivate yourself, think about this.

To me, school is a bit like a big fancy dress shop: you go in there and come out as anything you want to be!

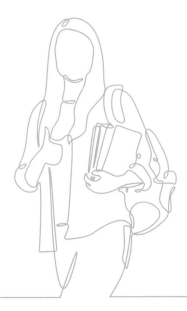

MY DREAM JOB

Use this page to write down some of your career ambitions. You can note down as many ideas as you like, or – if you have one dream job in mind – write about how you might start working towards your career goal.

DON'T
WISH
FOR IT,
WORK
FOR IT

CHAPTER THREE

THINK BIG

> "IF YOU THINK YOU'RE TOO SMALL TO HAVE AN IMPACT,
> TRY GOING TO BED WITH A MOSQUITO IN THE ROOM."
>
> ANITA RODDICK, FOUNDER OF THE BODY SHOP AND
> ENVIRONMENTAL AND HUMAN RIGHTS CAMPAIGNER

This made me itch! But in this analogy, Anita was that mosquito. She was one tiny person in a big world, speaking out about things she was passionate about – and she made a huge impact!

Anita did something no one else was really doing on a large scale at the time and created a global brand of beauty products that weren't tested on animals. She wasn't frightened to "think big" and start a business that celebrated her values. Not only did she achieve a lot through her campaigning, but she also created a hugely successful multi-million-pound business.

POLITICAL THINKERS

In America there's something called the "American dream". This is basically the idea that anyone (from any social or economic background) can become whatever they want to be – even if that's the president of the United States. To date though, it is the UK, not America, that has had women leading their country.

Margaret Thatcher became our first female prime minister in 1979. Her rise to success was not due to her family's wealth, nor was it due to an elite education. What got Margaret the job were her own drive, determination and self-belief.

She earned a place at one of the best universities in the world, the University of Oxford, to study chemistry. This was quite an awesome achievement, because at that time not many women went to university at all, let alone to study a subject such as chemistry!

Later in her life, Margaret managed to break into the male-dominated world of politics and eventually became the British prime minister; it seems as though she embraced "thinking big". The fact that no other woman had done it before didn't daunt her. Being the first to do something you want to do shouldn't daunt you either. Theresa May was the UK's second female prime minister and, who knows, you could become just as successful in politics too, if that's what you want!

All around the world there have been women who have made history by being the first or the youngest to do something – but they would probably never have got there if they hadn't first thought big.

In New Zealand, Jacinda Ardern recently became the world's youngest female prime minister.

Years ago, Indira Gandhi in India and Benazir Bhutto in Pakistan became the first female leaders of their countries. Benazir Bhutto also became the youngest elected leader in the Islamic world. As if these facts weren't impressive enough, Jacinda Ardern and Benazir Bhutto both became mothers while serving as prime minister.

I'm telling you about these women because they're proof that even if something hasn't been done before, it doesn't mean it can't be achieved. You just need to think big.

YOUR ONLY LIMIT IS YOUR IMAGINATION

"NEVER BE LIMITED BY OTHER PEOPLE'S LIMITED IMAGINATIONS. IF YOU ADOPT THEIR ATTITUDES, THEN THE POSSIBILITY WON'T EXIST BECAUSE YOU'LL HAVE ALREADY SHUT IT OUT."

MAE JEMISON, FORMER NASA ASTRONAUT AND THE FIRST AFRICAN-AMERICAN WOMAN TO TRAVEL INTO SPACE

I CAN
AND
I WILL

Mae is clearly an incredible woman, and there are others like her in all kinds of different areas of work, like Sheryl Sandberg, Serena Williams, Arianna Huffington, Huda Kattan, Oprah Winfrey, J. K. Rowling, Cher Wang, Indra Nooyi and Martha Lane Fox. You might never have heard of some of these women, but they are all successful in their field and have excelled in their profession.

Some of these women came from poverty to achieve great things; some even suffered major setbacks along the way. However, all of these women have one thing in common: they all thought big.

Of all the women I've mentioned, the ones you'll probably know best are Serena Williams and J. K. Rowling. Serena is one of the world's most successful female athletes, playing tennis professionally. Even having a child hasn't stopped her from pursuing her passion of playing top-level tennis. J. K. Rowling is famous for writing the Harry Potter books, and she's also an incredibly successful writer of books for adults. She has sold 500 million copies of her Harry Potter books alone, in more than 80 languages!

Of course, excelling at whatever you choose to do isn't easy – it takes years of work – but both these women love what they do, and their passion helps them to succeed.

The other women I've mentioned in this chapter also have amazing stories. Although you may not instantly recognize their names, their individual journeys to success are eye-opening. They are certainly proof of the fact that your barriers to achieving something only exist because you put them there!

WHAT'S STOPPING YOU?

While all the women I've spoken about so far in this chapter have made their way to the top of their chosen professions, it seems that not enough women do. Often, it's not because they're not good enough, but because they lack the self-belief to make it as far as they're capable of going.

There are many different reasons for this. Some studies among women in the US have shown that men overestimate their abilities and performance, while women tend to underestimate both. '

A UK study of around 2,000 British women found many women had inhibitions about their appearance, and this self-doubt had a severe impact on how women acted in the workplace.

The important thing to note is, when women do get to the top (and don't let these sorts of things stop them) amazing things can happen! Not only are women good at what they do, but in some cases they are actually better than men! In 2016, The Peterson Institute for International Economics completed a survey of more than 21,000 firms in more than 90 countries and found that having women in leadership roles led to an increase in profits.

Throughout all of my working life, I have never once thought "I can't". When I decided I wanted to become a journalist, it never occurred to me that I wouldn't do it, or that as a woman I would be discriminated against; I just got on with it and kept moving forward until I achieved my goal. It wasn't easy and, at first, I got lots of rejection letters. But despite all that, I didn't give up – and you mustn't either.

Girls, I encourage you all to think big and go for those jobs that seem like they're out of reach. Apply for the promotions that are usually given to men. Unless you push your way forward and prove you can do these jobs, nothing will ever change or get easier for the women in the generations after you.

"I NEVER, EVER GREW UP AS A YOUNG WOMAN BELIEVING THAT MY GENDER WOULD STAND IN THE WAY OF DOING ANYTHING I WANTED."

JACINDA ARDERN, PRIME MINISTER OF NEW ZEALAND

WHAT'S STOPPING ME?

Use this page to write down some of the things you feel are standing in the way of you achieving your dreams. Then, write down all the ways you can think of to overcome these obstacles.

LEAD THE WAY!

Until a few years ago (in the UK and US), nurses were nearly always female, and doctors were mostly male. Thankfully this statistic has started to change. In the UK in 2017, there were more female than male doctors for the first time in the country's history. Also, in the US, more women than men were in medical school training to be doctors in 2019.

It also used to be the case that virtually all police officers were men. When women started to join the police force in the 1960s and 70s, they only had minor roles; today, women often hold very senior jobs in this sector. London's Metropolitan Police Service is run by Cressida Dick. In 2018 she said that she wanted half of London's officers to be female – at the time just 27 per cent were women.

Right now, around the world (and particularly in India, Poland, Liberia, Pakistan, Peru and Ghana), women police officers are leading the fight against serious crimes, including human trafficking and corruption. Some are even undertaking peacekeeping missions with the United Nations. Changes like this can happen if a few women decide to think big and join male-dominated professions. Their actions, plus changes in the law and changes to the way society generally sees women, encourage other women to create change with them. Slowly, societies across the world are coming to accept that women can do these jobs just as well as their male counterparts.

Don't be put off if you have to be a pioneer in your chosen career. Your actions today will encourage other women to follow in your footsteps.

There are people who will genuinely want to protect you from failure and will try to talk you out of "thinking big". These people are, in some ways, thinking of you; they're probably trying to be kind, as they know how much effort it will take, and they don't want you to be hurt should you get knocked back.

The reality is, we all suffer knock-backs and failures: it's a fact of life. Don't take rejection personally, and make sure you keep going. No one wants to look back on their life and think: "What if I had tried a bit harder? Perhaps I would've achieved my ambition".

Failure is not bad, but not trying something is. If you don't try, you'll never know if you can succeed!

BE A CHAMPION

UK Olympian Jessica Ennis-Hill trained for hours and hours a day because she wanted to win an Olympic gold medal and be the best in the world at her sport. By thinking big and putting in a lot of hard work (even though she suffered setbacks along the way), she made her ambition her reality.

The feeling of being up on that Olympic podium and being handed a gold medal in front of the whole world must have been truly incredible. Her hard work hasn't just earned her sporting glory, but fame and fortune too. In 2017 Jessica was made a dame during a ceremony at Buckingham Palace, for her services to athletics, and was handed the honour by Prince William. But getting to that awesome stage in her life wasn't easy.

> "I'M PROUD OF THE WAY I'VE DEALT WITH SETBACKS. IT'S HARD WHEN YOU FEEL DOWN AND YOU THINK, 'WHY IS THE WORLD DOING THIS TO ME?' BUT YOU HAVE TO PICK YOURSELF UP AGAIN. THAT'S WHAT MAKES YOU A BETTER ATHLETE."
>
> ## JESSICA ENNIS-HILL, DBE, ATHLETE AND OLYMPIC GOLD MEDALLIST

Jessica's sparkle and the fact she thought big – Olympic-gold-medal big! – helped her pick herself up when things didn't go right; this is a great lesson for us all.

SUCCESS IS A DECISION

Don't let people hold you back because they can't understand your big dream for your life, or because they want to protect you from any failures – sadly, failures and disappointment come to us all.

There is a phrase I really hate (that people use so often), which I really think does more harm than good: "be realistic". Though it's meant to be helpful, this phrase can actually be anything but that. What does "being realistic" really mean? When people use it, they tend to use it to dilute people's dreams.

If people were "realistic", we would never have made it to the moon, invented the internet, or pioneered medical organ transplants that save thousands of lives a year. It's the "unrealistic" people who get amazing things done; the people who make these things happen are the people who believe they can do something and then do it.

KEEP GOING

Girls, if we fail at something the first time, it's easy to just write ourselves off as useless and give up. What I'm telling you to do is to keep going. Virtually no successful person had success straight away – they learned from their mistakes and got there in the end. The key thing is that they didn't stop themselves from "thinking big".

> "EVEN AS FAR BACK AS WHEN I STARTED ACTING AT FOURTEEN, I KNOW I'VE NEVER CONSIDERED FAILURE."

JENNIFER LAWRENCE, AMERICAN ACTOR

Jennifer Lawrence knew what she wanted, and she went and got it – her mindset was positive. If you put your mind into "can do" mode, you too can achieve your big dream. You may not want to be a Hollywood star or run an international business – that doesn't matter – but by thinking big, you are capable of achieving whatever your dream is.

Our minds are really powerful when it comes to whether we achieve our dreams or not. If we think we can't do something we tend to fail at it, but if we think we can do something then we tend to achieve it. You probably know this already from things you've experienced, like when you're doing sports and stop too long to think, for example: "Can I really run and jump over that hurdle in one go? It looks a bit high!" It's not your ability but your doubt that stops you. However, if you didn't stop to think about it and just went for it, you would probably clear the hurdle easily.

Your mind can have an incredible effect on your ability to achieve. Put positive things in your mind, and you will get positive things out; put negative things in, and doubt follows – which could kill off your progress right there and then!

We all know we can talk ourselves in and out of things if we think too long about them. If we're not careful, we can sabotage ourselves by thinking we can't do something before we've even tried! Instead let's use that brainpower to think positively about how we're going to do something – not whether we might fail!

> "WHAT WE FIND IS THAT IF YOU HAVE A GOAL THAT IS VERY, VERY FAR OUT, AND YOU APPROACH IT IN LITTLE STEPS, YOU START TO GET THERE FASTER. YOUR MIND OPENS UP TO THE POSSIBILITIES."
>
> ## MAE JEMISON

You're young, and at this age you can work toward being anything you want and achieving anything you want to. All you have to do is decide what you want from life and then slowly and steadily work toward getting it. It really is that simple.

> "NO PESSIMIST EVER DISCOVERED THE SECRET OF THE STARS, OR SAILED TO AN UNCHARTED LAND, OR OPENED A NEW DOORWAY FOR THE HUMAN SPIRIT."

HELEN KELLER, AMERICAN AUTHOR, LECTURER, POLITICAL ACTIVIST AND THE FIRST DEAF-BLIND PERSON TO EARN A BACHELOR OF ARTS DEGREE

Helen was awesome and definitely wasn't afraid to think big! Her achievements are absolutely mind-blowing. Born in 1880, Helen fell ill and was left deaf and blind by the age of just two. You might think that that would have been it for her – that her life would have been pretty much over. However, this was only the start of a difficult but truly inspirational journey. Her family and her teacher never gave up on her. Vitally, she also never gave up on herself.

Helen spent 25 years learning to speak clearly again (so that others could understand her), and she then became a passionate campaigner for women's rights and social justice. She travelled all around the world to help others.

Helen had a remarkable life, and she didn't let her disabilities stop her. I can't think of many other humans who have endured so much but who have been so determined to triumph over adversity. When I think I can't do something, or that it's too hard, I just think of Helen and pick myself back up to try again.

Don't put up barriers to what you can achieve in your life. Someone always has to be the first to achieve something – why can't it be you?

WHAT'S STOPPING ME?

Use this page to write down some of the things you feel are standing in the way of you achieving your dreams. Then, write down all the ways you can think of to overcome these obstacles.

_____

_____

_____

_____

_____

_____

_____

_____

_____

_____

_____

_____

_____

_____

_____

_____

_____

_____

_____

_____

_____

YOUR DREAMS ARE ACHIEVABLE

CHAPTER FOUR

BEING AWESOME

When you think about someone who's awesome, you probably think of someone who has achieved great things – someone you admire and look up to. Perhaps you love sport, so Olympic gold medallist and gymnast Simone Biles is totally awesome to you. Perhaps you admire the singer-songwriter Billie Eilish, who not only has an amazing talent for making music but also embraces her own unique style and femininity. Or perhaps you love TV and films, and the Oscar-nominated actor and singer Cynthia Erivo would be at the top of your "awesome person" list.

Then there are people who end up making a big difference in the world and who change people's lives for the better. Maybe you look up to Michelle Obama, who spends a lot of her time travelling around the globe, inspiring young girls to achieve their dreams. Or maybe you admire Malala Yousafzai, who was shot in her country (Pakistan) for going to school but survived and is now fighting for other girls to have the right to an education.

These women may be very different in lots of ways, but they are all awesome.

There are many types of "awesome" and being awesome doesn't mean you have to be rich or famous. Some of the most awesome people in this world are people who dedicate their lives to helping others, like teachers, firefighters, doctors, paramedics and carers. Awesome people are also those who invent things that can change lives, and those who put other people first even though their own lives are hard.

WHAT DOES "AWESOME" REALLY MEAN?

The dictionary tells us that "awesome" means being "extremely impressive", "amazing" and "causing feelings of respect or great admiration". This definition certainly fits all the women I've just mentioned. But can you really be awesome too?

NOW
IS THE TIME
TO BE
AWESOME

The answer to that is yes. Being awesome is not a superpower, and it's not something you have to wait to have until you are grown up or have a great career. It's a collection of attributes that we can all have if we work at them and that can help power us through our whole lives, helping us to achieve whatever we want to.

So, here's a starting point for how you can bring out your inner awesome:

ONE

BE KIND

This is my favourite tip because of the uplifting effect it has: not only does being kind help other people, but it makes you feel great too. Kindness never goes unnoticed, and it can really make a difference in people's lives. Whether it's offering a kind word when someone is feeling down, encouraging them, or helping someone carry bags or do a chore, it's the little things like this that can make a big difference to people. If I could pick only one tip, I would choose this. The only caveat to this is to make sure people don't take advantage of your kindness. Remember: kindness isn't a weakness – it's a strength. Just because you are kind that doesn't mean you have to be a pushover.

TWO

BE YOURSELF

At school and when we're young, there is a great deal of pressure on us to fit in. But don't be so focused on fitting in that you become someone else. If you have a unique style – maybe you like dressing a certain way, or maybe you have hair that's very different from those around you – embrace it! Don't change it or hide it just because you feel you should look and act like everyone else. If you love it, flaunt it. To be honest, your friends and schoolmates will probably think you're quite cool, because you're brave enough to go against the so-called "norm" and be who you are.

Maybe you love a particular type of music that is way different from your friends (or other people your age) – don't be afraid to say so. You might get a reputation for being "quirky", but that's no bad thing. Always remain true to yourself, your values and your standards; part of being awesome is not changing who you are to fit in. Embrace the things that make you you. If everyone was the same, what a dull and boring world we would live in.

THREE
BE POSITIVE

Being a positive thinker helps with managing stress levels. It's good for your health and it's the sort of quality other people notice and find really attractive. If you're a "glass-half-full" person rather than a "glass-half-empty" person, you can problem-solve much more easily. I don't know a single pessimistic person who has achieved amazing things – it's always the positive thinkers who get on with things. Positive people have a good energy around them, and tend to attract similar people too.

FOUR
BE CONFIDENT

This doesn't mean that you should be really boastful or go around telling everyone how great you are. Just believe in your heart that you're an awesome girl who can do anything she puts her mind to. Have faith in yourself, because if you do, then others will – and that's when amazing things can happen.

FIVE
USE YOUR TALENTS

If you're good at something, don't hide it. Maybe you can sing or play a musical instrument; maybe you're good at acting or love public speaking; maybe you speak a second language – these are all awesome talents, so show them off! Don't show off in an annoying way by bragging, but also don't be afraid to sign yourself up for opportunities that allow you to showcase your talent, whether that's a gig, a school performance, or joining the school sports team. These skills may become much more than hobbies and they could even end up being your career! By showing off your talents, you shine.

SIX

You're a very special person. Sometimes life gets tiring and we must remember to take care of ourselves physically in order to support our mental health. It may mean taking time to be alone and doing simple things, like staying in and watching a TV show you love, cooking something, tidying your room, or reading a book. Perhaps you could also try taking a hot bath to help you sleep well at night. A good night's sleep means that you'll wake up refreshed and ready for the day ahead. Get up early so you have time to have a shower and decide what to wear before you go to school or college; if we look good, we feel good. I don't mean you should be vain, just that you should take pride in yourself. The way we look is the first thing people notice about us. Personally, I couldn't leave the house without spraying a nice smell on myself – it gives me a boost and makes me feel good. Don't just make an effort on special occasions – every day is special! We all notice when someone takes care of their appearance, and by doing so you're sending out the message that you value yourself. When you value yourself, others will value you too.

SEVEN

FORGIVE

Don't hold grudges because they will eat away at you and make you unhappy. If someone has upset you, tell them they've hurt you and why. If the person is reasonable, they will probably want to say sorry and make it up to you; if they don't, you can always walk away and find better friends. The way you stand up for yourself and the way you treat others makes you stand out in life. Often, people fall out over nothing, which is pointless. Life is beautiful but short, so don't lose friends over silly arguments. Of course, if you're at fault, be the bigger person and apologize.

EIGHT

DON'T GET PUSHED ABOUT

While we should value other people's opinions, we shouldn't let them diminish our dreams. Deep down we know what we're capable of, so ignore the doubters and plough on. Don't crush people on your path to success, but as long as your dreams aren't harming anyone, carry right on and prove them wrong. Belief in yourself is awesome.

NINE

BE GRATEFUL

Try to think about what is good in your life and be thankful for it on a daily basis. Something amazing might have happened to you, such as receiving a lovely gift from a friend, or winning a competition – but it's not just material things we should value and appreciate. Be grateful too for the people in your life, your friends and family, and be thankful for your pets. Those who remember to be grateful for the things in their life that most people take for granted tend to have a more positive outlook. Remember to tell people that you're grateful for the things they do for you – it will make them so happy to know you appreciate them.

TEN

LAUGH AND BE HAPPY

It's so nice to be around happiness and laughter; just hearing someone laugh is infectious. Sharing a joke makes us happy and lifts our mood, and we're naturally attracted to happy people, as they appear more confident. Plus, it really is true that laughter is the best medicine: scientists have found that laughter can relieve stress. So, go on – have a giggle!

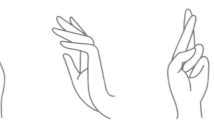

UNCOVERING MY INNER AWESOME

Use this page to note down some of your favourite tips from the list, as well as any other ways you can think of to bring out the awesome inside you!

_____

_____

_____

_____

_____

_____

_____

_____

_____

_____

_____

_____

_____

_____

_____

_____

_____

_____

_____

_____

_____

LEARN TO LOVE YOURSELF

Constantly worrying that we are too fat, too thin, too short or too tall can throw us off track in life. We need to like – or at least accept – what we see in the mirror. Don't dwell on what you would rather see there. We're all different shapes and sizes. As a teenager, your body is going to be changing for a while yet, so don't be obsessed with it. The most important thing we can do for our bodies is to stay healthy, exercise and eat well.

Everyone – but especially women and girls – go through times where they dislike certain things about themselves. However, the important thing to remember is that the things we think of as our "bad bits" are rarely even noticed by our friends (or anyone else, for that matter). Often, we blow these things way out of proportion – and that's if they even exist!

Look back at the list of awesome women I mentioned at the start of this chapter. These women all look very different. Being awesome is not about looks, size or shape. How you are as a person is what makes you truly awesome. When we realize this, we can take a lot of pressure off ourselves, and instead invest that energy into all the things I've been talking about here.

To help you like or accept yourself as you are, try this exercise. Look at yourself in a mirror and say what you like about your looks. You might be thinking: "That's easy: not a lot!" But I'm sure that's not true. Look again. Come up with at least three things. It could be that you like your eyes, your hair, or your smile. If you come up with more than three, great!

Now stand away from the mirror and think about what you like about your personality. Are you fun to be around? Are you kind? Are you thoughtful? These are all things that really make you attractive and likeable to those around you.

LOVING MYSELF

Use this page to write down all the things you love about yourself. Make sure you include lots of positive thoughts about your personality, as well as your appearance.

I'm sure the mirror scenario and the notes page here will take some of you ages to do, but if I asked you to tell me what's attractive about your best friend, you would probably reel off a list straight away – and that's brilliant, because I bet your best friend would do the same for you! Try it; it'll make you both feel good.

"LEARNING TO BE GRATEFUL FOR OUR BODIES AND TAKING CARE OF THEM ARE THE BEST WAYS FOR US TO EMPOWER OURSELVES PHYSICALLY, MENTALLY AND SPIRITUALLY."

DEMI LOVATO, AMERICAN SINGER-SONGWRITER, ACTOR AND TV PERSONALITY

Demi is right, but at school image can be seen as everything. Puberty can be cruel: we get hairy, start our periods and get spots. Just remember that everyone else is going through it too. Some may sail through this time in their lives more easily than others, but that doesn't mean they'll avoid it completely.

PRIORITIZE YOUR SKILLS

We live in a world that tells us to look a certain way if we want to be liked, and that can make us feel anything but awesome. Take the music industry: it's often the female music artists who are seen wearing virtually nothing. Is this the same for males in the industry?

Interestingly, Adele, who never wears skimpy clothes on stage, has turned out to be one of the world's most successful singers. She's definitely awesome, because she never bought into society's idea that she had to look a certain way to be attractive and successful. She has her own unique style and it suits her. Though her style and her look have changed as she's grown older, she never set out to conform.

"I MAKE MUSIC TO BE A MUSICIAN, NOT TO BE ON THE COVER OF *PLAYBOY*."

ADELE, MBE, ENGLISH SINGER-SONGWRITER

Worrying about looks all the time is bad for us. A test carried out by American psychologists showed that worrying about how we look can really hold us back and stop us performing at our best.

In this experiment (which aimed to find out how body image can affect boys and girls differently), researchers asked both male and female college students to try on either a jumper or swimwear. Once dressed, they asked the students to sit a maths test. The results revealed that the girls wearing swimsuits did much worse in the tests than those wearing sweaters; they were more worried about how they looked in the swimwear to perform at their best on the test. Surprisingly, there were no differences for the young men.*

Another study looked at the "throwing like a girl" stereotype. The study** found that compared to boys, girls tended not to bring their whole bodies into a throw. This wasn't because they couldn't, but because these girls (aged 10–17) were so concerned about how their bodies would look if they did, they didn't put their all into the throw.

This, again, shows that a lack of body confidence – or thinking we have to look a certain way all the time – can lead to us underperforming; this stops us being awesome.

The funny thing is that if you put your all into a throw, you will probably throw it well, and if you do that then no one will be noticing how you look – they'll be thinking how good you are at throwing!

* Report of the American Psychological Association Task Force on the Sexualization of Girls (2010)

** "Throwing Like a Girl: Self-Objectification Predicts Adolescent Girls' Motor Performance", Fredrickson and Harrison (2005)

WHAT ARE MY SKILLS?

Use this page to record all the amazing skills you have, as well as any skills that you would like to develop. If you can, try to think of some things you could do to develop the skills you'd like to work on.

> "THINK OF ALL THE GIRLS WHO COULD BECOME TOP ATHLETES BUT QUIT SPORTS BECAUSE THEY'RE AFRAID OF HAVING TOO MANY DEFINED MUSCLES AND BEING MADE FUN OF OR CALLED UNATTRACTIVE."

SERENA WILLIAMS

Serena makes a brilliant point.

SEXISM ISN'T AWESOME

Another thing that can really hold us back, undermine us and stop us from feeling awesome is a sexist attitude.

A report by Girlguiding in the UK said that girls identified sexism as something that affected most areas of their lives. And the UK children's charity NSPCC reported that there is a "deeply rooted notion that girls and young women's bodies are somehow the property of boys and young men".

This is mind-blowingly awful!

This isn't just a problem in the UK, either. In the US, Australia and Europe, studies and reports are showing that sexism is still a big worry for girls and women.

A 2018 study by a group of American universities showed that the effects of sexist beliefs on women's abilities (and the sort of jobs and roles they went on to have in life) affected their socio-economic status. In other words, women tend to earn less because of the jobs they are led to do. The study also revealed that the area where they grew up could have a negative effect on a woman's sense of self. They found that if sexism was a problem in the state where the woman was born, then even if the woman moved to another area, she will probably still live her life having been affected by the values she grew up with.*

* "The Effects of Sexism on American Women: The Role of Norms vs Discrimination" (2018)

In Australia, a study by the *Journal of Applied Social Psychology* showed that workplace sexism lessened a woman's sense of belonging as it symbolized a form of bullying, ostracism and rejection by men. It also led to women feeling alienated and lonely.

This shows the devastating effect that sexism can have. Sexism can stop you from being your awesome self because it makes you feel inferior. It can make you feel like an object rather than a human being with thoughts and emotions. Sadly, sexist language is all around us; in pop music, for example, the words "bitches" and "hoes" are often used to refer to girls. Unfortunately, this sort of language has now crept into everyday language in schools too.

At school, you should feel empowered and safe, but girls in the UK are reporting that they're being subjected to sexual assault and verbal abuse.

One girl (aged 13), at a school in the UK, told researchers that she could not expect to walk past boys in the school corridor without them touching her – either squeezing her bum or touching her boobs.*

It's very hard to feel awesome if this is something you're facing at school. No girl should have to go through this anywhere. If this is happening to you and your friends at school, you must report it at home, at school and to the police. Sexual assault is a crime. Please don't be frightened to tell someone, because if you don't say anything, it will very likely just continue.

I know that talking to a parent or a trusted adult about this can be scary, but if you feel you can't speak face to face to them, you can always write it down and leave them a note – or even email them. Trust me: they will want to know, and they will want to help.

* "A Qualitative Study of Children, Young People and Sexting" by the NSPCC and the London School of Economics (2012)

Being brave and standing up to sexism is an awesome thing to do, but you don't have to do it all by yourself. If it's a problem in your school, talk to other girls and decide what you want to do about it. Maybe you'd feel better if you reported the problem as a group? Perhaps you could suggest that the teachers hold an assembly to discuss the problem with the whole school? Or maybe you could set up a "zero tolerance on sexism" campaign.

Lots of boys won't have thought much about how their name-calling or sexist behaviour makes you feel, so tell them. They're young too and might only just be learning about how to treat girls and how to have relationships. Educate them into behaving more appropriately toward women. Even better, get them to join the campaign!

Being awesome is all the things I've talked about here (and more!). Ultimately though, it's that quiet inner peace and belief in yourself that you can cope with life's ups and downs that make you awesome. You already have all the qualities you need inside you, so don't be afraid to show them to the world!

GREAT THINGS NEVER CAME FROM COMFORT ZONES

CHAPTER FIVE

SELF-ESTEEM

Self-esteem means feeling good about yourself. A lack of self-esteem can leave us feeling sad or – even worse – depressed and anxious.

When you're growing up, your self-esteem is especially fragile. This is because you're still working out who you are and who you want to be. If someone is nasty to you, or you fail at something, you can easily be crushed by it – and this can dent or kill your self-esteem entirely.

So, how do you know if you have low self-esteem? Well, these are pretty clear signs:

ONE
You feel down and generally bad about yourself.

TWO
You think you're not good enough.

THREE
You beat yourself up over little things when they go wrong.

Having high self-esteem is the feeling that you are worthy of good things. It's about valuing yourself and it's about believing that you have a value in society.

If you have good self-esteem you tend to:

ONE
Feel you are good enough.

TWO
Believe in yourself and your abilities.

THREE
Feel good generally, and feel that you're liked and accepted by friends and family.

If you agreed with the first three statements rather than the last three, don't worry: we'll work on it.

HOW DO I FEEL ABOUT MYSELF?

Use this page to explore how you feel about yourself at this moment, and think about how these thoughts may affect your self-esteem. Return to this page once you've finished this chapter, and reflect on the things you have written down. Use the page opposite to note down all the things you could do to improve your self-esteem.

The sad thing is that it's not always other people who bring us down – sometimes we're just unkind to ourselves. If we don't do well in a test, for example, we can brand ourselves as a loser. In reality, we should reassure ourselves it was just one test and next time we will very likely do better.

As girls, there is also a lot of pressure to look, and behave, in a certain way. Society tells us that if we're slim with perfect skin, we're somehow better people; having good self-esteem means you know that this isn't true. Everyone is different. We're different heights, shapes and sizes; we're different colours; we have different hair and features. One type of look isn't better than another. Our differences are what make us special and they should be celebrated.

I can't reinforce this enough: having good self-esteem is not about how you look, but how you feel and what kind of person you are.

Here are my top tips for good self-esteem:

ONE

KNOW THAT YOU DESERVE GOOD THINGS: understand that you're a good person and you deserve to be treated with respect. Know that you have a place in this world and that you matter. Treat others like this too.

TWO

STOP BEING SO HARD ON YOURSELF: if you only get five out of ten in a test, for example, acknowledge the "failure" and move on. If this wasn't your best effort, tell yourself that next time you will do better. Don't keep beating yourself up over it as this is likely to make you worse at whatever it is you feel you've done badly at! Be as compassionate and kind to yourself as you would be to a friend in the same situation.

THREE

CELEBRATE YOUR SUCCESSES: allow yourself to be pleased when you do well at something. It might be something fairly small, like baking a delicious cake that everyone compliments you on, but that doesn't matter. Soak up the compliments and let yourself enjoy them. You're allowed to be proud of yourself.

FOUR

SEIZE NEW OPPORTUNITIES: say yes to things that might push you out of your comfort zone but that you know deep down you'd like to try. Doing new things can give you a real buzz.

FIVE

VALUE YOURSELF: don't be afraid to say no to people if they want you to do something you don't want to do. Being able to do this really makes you feel good – believe me! Take control and see how liberating it can be.

SIX

HELP SOMEONE ELSE: maybe you're really good at a certain subject and your friend isn't – perhaps you could help them! Helping other people always makes us feel good, and it makes the person we're helping feel good too.

SEVEN

STOP COMPARING YOURSELF TO OTHERS: it's enough to do your very best. It's likely that someone will always be better at something than you, so don't try to compete with that – just do as well as you can and be pleased when you improve. Remember you're probably better than them at something else.

EIGHT

NOURISH YOUR BODY: ditch the junk and add some healthy foods into your diet – good food feeds the brain. Too much sugar and fat can leave us feeling tired and sluggish.

NINE

DITCH THE HATERS: if your friends and the people you hang out with don't make you feel good about yourself, ditch them. Find people who make you feel good, and don't cling on to people just because they're the "in crowd". If anyone makes you feel lousy, they're not a nice person – so move on!

These tips should make you feel better about yourself. Read them as often as you like, and put them into practice too.

MAKE YOURSELF A PRIORITY

DEPRESSION

Having good self-esteem is so important because it can really help to protect our mental health. If you have rock bottom self-esteem and it's not identified and treated, it can lead to depression.

Recently, a UK-government-funded study found that one in four girls are depressed at the age of 14. Their symptoms included feeling miserable, tired, lonely and hating themselves. This is hideous.

Although boys suffer with depression too, it's been found that girls are more than twice as likely to be diagnosed with this kind of mood disorder. It's thought that it could be because girls mature at a younger age than boys.

In the UK, about 166,000 girls and 67,000 boys are depressed.

Across Europe, statistics show pretty much the same thing.

In America, seven out of ten teenagers listed depression and anxiety as major problems in their lives.

If you're feeling depressed, you're likely to have some – or all – of these symptoms:

ONE   Feeling lethargic and sleeping too much or not enough.

TWO   Loss of appetite or eating way too much.

THREE   No interest in seeing friends or doing any of the fun things you used to like to do.

FOUR   Feeling worthless and helpless.

FIVE   Feeling you can't concentrate in lessons.

Understanding what you're feeling is a great step toward getting better. Confide in someone; you can overcome these feelings, but you will need to open up and ask for help. Talk to your friend or parent or another trusted adult. It is also advisable that you seek professional help.

If you spot that a friend is struggling, here are a few things you can do to help them:

ONE   Talk to them and listen to what they have to say. Really listening to how they feel is important.

TWO   Remind them that you are there for them.

THREE   Suggest that they talk to their parents or a trusted adult – or call one of the many hotlines where they can get professional advice.*

FOUR   Do not tell them to cheer up. It won't help them if you say that because depression is an illness.

FIVE   Ask them if there's anything you can do to help to make them feel better.

SIX   Tell a trusted adult or a teacher that you are concerned about their well-being.

Help is out there – please don't be afraid to ask for it. It doesn't make you weak or weird. Asking for help when you need it is a strength. By asking for help, you're looking after yourself – and that's really positive!

ANXIETY

This leads me to anxiety. Anxiety can be feeling worried about a range of everyday things, or it could be something that has been triggered by one big thing that you've experienced.

* There are some resources for you at the back of this book

Anxiety is a natural reaction to stress, and it can make you feel really rough. It's a feeling of nervousness but to such an extent that it overwhelms you and you no longer feel in control of a situation. It can make you feel on edge and panicky.

It's a common feeling, and experts say around one in five young people are anxious from time to time.

You'll know if you have anxiety because it tends to trigger a wide range of symptoms that can be anything from feeling you can't breathe to feeling sick or getting stomach aches. You may even get diarrhoea and feel the need to rush to the bathroom. You may feel hot, sweaty and shaky.

Sometimes anxiety may not be quite this overwhelming. You may be able to function, but just not be at your best. You may find yourself constantly feeling a bit on edge, biting your nails all the time, scratching and picking at your skin, scratching your scalp or pulling out strands of your hair.

There are some great apps that you can download to help with anxiety but there are lots of things you can do yourself too. Here are just a few:

ONE

BREATHE: I know this will sound crazy because we all breathe, don't we? What I mean by this is really breathe. Close your mouth and take a deep breath in through your nose; fill your lungs, and then when you can't take any more, slowly breathe out through your mouth. Concentrate on this action, taking big breaths in and then slowly out. Hear yourself breathing. Repeat this at least three times, or until you feel calmer.

TWO

TAKE YOURSELF SOMEWHERE CALM AND QUIET: removing yourself from whatever is creating a surge in your anxiety levels should help you feel calm almost immediately.

THREE

WRITE YOUR FEARS AND WORRIES DOWN: seeing your worries in black and white can help to focus you and help you to work through them. It might even show you that they're not as big as you had first thought – in fact, this is very often the case.

FOUR

EXERCISE: regular exercise is so good for our mental health because it releases chemicals that naturally improve how we feel. So, get outside; go for a walk or, even better, a run. If you can't go out for any reason, stay inside and dance to your favourite music – go until you get your heart rate up and are out of breath. If you want to know the science bit: getting your heart rate up releases endorphins (happy hormones), which help counter stress and negative feelings.

FIVE

TALK TO SOMEONE YOU TRUST ABOUT WHAT IS MAKING YOU FEEL ANXIOUS: this is so important. It could be a friend, a teacher or your mum or dad, but make sure you find someone you trust and tell them how you're feeling. Try to talk to a medical professional if you can. Sharing is good, because often what we feel anxious about can easily be sorted out with the right support around us.

WHAT ARE MY WORRIES?

If you ever feel anxious, use this page to write down your worries. As explained above, getting your thoughts onto paper can help you to get a sense of perspective. Perhaps you'll realize things aren't as bad as they seem!

Lack of self-esteem, depression and anxiety are not things to be embarrassed about. However, we should be aware that these conditions can end up holding us back in life. Having good mental health is really important not only because it helps us maintain our physical health, but also because we can't reach our full, awesome potential without it. The good news is that you can get help for mental health conditions, which can help you to manage the symptoms, as well as put you on the right footing toward recovery.

What I hope you will remember (because it is absolutely true) is that you are an awesome and unique person. You are good enough. You don't have to be like everyone else to fit in. There is no other person on the planet like you, and that makes you very special indeed.

THERE IS ONLY ONE YOU, AND THAT IS YOUR

SUPER POWER

CHAPTER SIX

IDENTITY

Gender identity is about your sense of who you are as a person, and it doesn't have to be based on whether or not you have boobs, a vagina or a menstrual cycle.

In general terms, it's our genitalia and our "biological differences" that define our "sex" and make us either female or male. However, our "gender" is a bit more difficult to define. Everyone has their own view of themselves. While a majority of people do identify with the sex they're born with and feel that they are that gender, others struggle to see themselves as the gender they've been assigned.

Gender identity is very complex, and there are lots of categories and terms for the way people identify; of course, some prefer not to use labels at all, and that's fine too! The important thing to remember here is: if you experience any of the feelings discussed in this chapter, you are not alone.

GENDER IN THE SPOTLIGHT

As soon as we're born – often even before then – our gender identity is usually defined for us. When someone has a baby, or even when a woman is still pregnant, the first thing we tend to ask is: "Is it a boy or a girl?" When we're born, a quick look at our reproductive organs leads to us being assigned a sex – either male or female – but as we grow up, it doesn't mean we always feel we are that gender.

Nowadays, it's getting easier to admit that you don't fit into the gender stereotypes we're used to. There's little doubt that this has been helped by young celebrities coming out and being open about their own gender identities.

When British singer-songwriter Sam Smith said, "I'm not male or female. I think I float somewhere in between", it helped to normalize different identities and helped start a conversation about gender and what that really means.

Sam is not alone in questioning society's common standards around identity and sexuality. American singer-songwriter and actor Miley Cyrus has openly said she is gender-fluid and that she doesn't feel like a girl or a boy.

> "I THINK ABOUT BEING A GIRL ALL THE TIME. I'M ALWAYS LIKE, 'IT'S WEIRD THAT I'M A GIRL BECAUSE I JUST DON'T FEEL LIKE A GIRL, AND I DON'T FEEL LIKE A BOY'."

MILEY CYRUS, AMERICAN SINGER-SONGWRITER AND ACTOR

American singer and actor Amandla Stenberg identifies as non-binary, while model and actor Cara Delevingne identifies as gender-fluid, and the model and actor Ruby Rose has also openly talked about being gender-fluid.

PINK FOR GIRLS AND BLUE FOR BOYS?

In children's clothes shops and in toy stores there's often a clear demarcation between "pink things" for girls and "blue things" for boys. Society – even in this day and age – seems to have quite a "pink vs blue" view of what children should enjoy and prefer based on their gender. Common thinking seems to be along the binary that boys are tough and loud, and don't wear skirts or make-up, while girls are quiet and caring, and do wear skirts and make-up.

Funnily enough though, the "pink is for girls and blue is for boys" phenomenon only started in the 1940s. Around 100 years ago, blue was seen as a "girl's colour" and pink was most often worn by boys. Though this is totally the opposite of today's view, it goes to show that some form of gender stereotyping has always been the norm!

If you go even further back, to the 1800s, white was the colour considered appropriate for all babies; children wore white, and both boys and girls wore dresses until the age of six or seven – which no one thought was weird!

DON'T TRADE AUTHENTICITY FOR APPROVAL

Clearly, attitudes about how boys and girls "should look" change over time. Maybe now society is ready for another change – one where people can dress their babies in any colour, or let their children wear what they want to wear, without being judged for it!

I want you to remember that you are you, and only you know how you feel, and how you want to dress.

BE TRUE TO YOURSELF

You may be reading this and thinking that you don't feel you fit the gender identity you were assigned at birth, or you may be thinking, "No, I'm definitely female, and I'm very happy with that identity". Whichever it is, there's no right and wrong. As a young person, your teenage years are when you will start to really question and uncover who you are, and there's no need to be frightened or ashamed of what you find.

Working out your identity and how you want to identify can be hard enough to do but working out how to fit into the world around you when you've decided that can be a very stressful experience. At school, you may be worried about how you'll be treated. Thankfully, a lot of schools now understand the need to help people with different gender identities fit in, so they try to make life as easy as possible for them. If you're concerned, talk to someone at your school: perhaps a teacher you like or, if your school has one, a counsellor. Many schools also have lessons on gender identity; these lessons should help your classmates better understand any changes you feel you want to make. You may want to change what you wear; you may want to change your name; and you may decide you want to be called "they" instead of "she". Your school should help you do all of these things. If you feel you need help to explain your feelings, there are lots of places you can go for help (I've listed a few resources at the back of this book).

Some people feel as though they're in the wrong body, and they might strongly identify with the opposite gender to the one they have been assigned. This is not common, but if you feel this way and your feelings are very intense, make sure you talk to your parents or a trusted adult about your feelings, and seek advice from your doctor. These are very complex feelings and you will need help to make sense of them. Some people will decide – with expert guidance – to go down the route of transitioning from female to male. They will have surgery and take hormones to do this. People who do this often identify as transsexuals. This is a long process and one that requires long-term medical treatment and support. **This change is not to be entered into lightly,** but with proper professional help, people are able to make an informed decision that is right for them.

Whatever you feel about your identity, you may also be worried about how to tell your friends and family. Although you might not believe it, you will feel better when you've told them. Bottling things up can make us really ill.

If you're worried about the reaction at home or from friends, call free helplines or look at the many websites run by charities where you live. All of these avenues will be able to offer you some good advice about how you might talk to your family and friends about what you're going through. They could also help you work through your feelings.

Talking to someone who's able to offer expert advice is really important. Don't try to struggle with complicated feelings alone, because you may start to feel isolated and worried about how you'll cope. These feelings could develop into depression and anxiety (see Chapter Five) and these are things that no one wants to have to go through.

The most important thing is to know that you're not alone, and that other young people also feel like this. There'll no doubt be lots of stuff whizzing through your mind about how and when to tell people if you're experiencing these feelings. So, here are just a few things to consider before you make that move:

ONE

GET EXPERT ADVICE: if possible, this should be your first step. Seek advice from a medical professional or from a charity that specializes in these issues. Once you've made sense of your feelings, you can better explain them to others.

TWO

THINK ABOUT WHEN AND WHERE YOU WILL RAISE THE SUBJECT: try to pick a quiet time when you can talk one to one with a parent, sibling or family member who you think will be sympathetic. Once you've told another person, they might be able to help you tell others in the family – and this can make things easier for you.

THREE

UNDERSTAND THAT THE PERSON YOU TELL MAY NOT UNDERSTAND WHAT YOU ARE SAYING AT FIRST, SO BE CLEAR: perhaps write down something that simply says how you feel and how you want to be treated as a result.

FOUR

BE PATIENT: depending on your family, their culture or religious beliefs, it may take them a while to get their heads around what you're saying.

FIVE

TRY NOT TO SHUT ANYONE OUT: some people may feel shock or sadness when you first tell them. Try to understand that although they may have these feelings initially, it doesn't mean they love you any less. They're probably just trying to work out what it all means – just like you did when you first understood your feelings.

LOOKING OUT FOR MYSELF AND OTHERS

Use this page to note down any thoughts you have about your identity, and how you would like to address them. Alternatively, note down all the ways you could support someone around you struggling with their identity.

Even if you're not dealing with any of these issues yourself, don't forget to look out for and be there for any friends or family members who you think may be going through them and might be struggling with how they feel. Remember they're probably dreading telling people around them. They might think that no one they know will understand, so a friendly face and sympathetic ear will be a great support for them.

Here are a few things you can do if you think someone is worrying about their gender identity, or things you can say if they open up to you:

ONE

Thank them for sharing it with you because it will have taken a lot of courage for them to do so.

TWO

Ask how you can support them. They may, for instance, want to be called by a different name, or they may want to change the pronoun people use to refer to them.

THREE

Ask how they feel about telling others about their gender identity and if you can help with that. Of course, you should never tell anyone without the person's permission.

FOUR

Ask questions as they will probably be keen to tell you. A conversation like this can help you better understand them and make them feel accepted.

FIVE

Carry on as normal. Don't change how you are with them. You are their friend for a reason – perhaps because you share lots of interests, or you enjoy their company – so keep treating them just as you did before the "big" announcement.

These are the small things you can do that will make a big difference. Gender identity and how someone chooses to live their life (and how they want to be treated as a result of that) may seem strange or shocking to hear about, but it doesn't change who a person is.

One of the best tips for life I've ever been given is that we should always treat people as we would want to be treated ourselves. Kindness is one of the best personality traits anyone can have. If we want to live in a happy and caring world, it starts with us. Remember: our differences are what make us awesome and unique.

RELATIONSHIPS

When you've worked out who you are, you might then be wondering who you're attracted to, and how to navigate the world of relationships.

What's it like to have a boyfriend or girlfriend, and to pucker up for that first lingering kiss? The butterflies you get in your tummy and the racing of your heart when you even just talk to someone you like can be thrilling.

There are many different types of love: love for your parents, your brothers and sisters, love for your best mates, etc. But these are all very different from the kind of love we feel in a romantic relationship. Love we feel in a romantic relationship tends to be love that involves a sexual attraction.

Romantic feelings usually develop during puberty – starting from around age 11 – and grow throughout our teenage years. You're likely to suddenly get passionate feelings of attraction for someone – feelings that you've never had before. It's a natural part of growing up. And although it can be exciting, these feelings can be confusing at first.

FIND
SOMEONE WHO
UNDERSTANDS
HOW SPECIAL
YOUR LOVE
IS

When you do feel this first rush of sexual attraction, it's easy to get swept away and totally consumed by the object of your desire, perhaps to the point where you can barely concentrate on anything else!

So, what's this romance thing all about? How can you make sure you are in a good and kind relationship, and what should you expect from romance?

FIRST LOVE

Not all that long ago, there was no internet, no social media and there were no smartphones. (I know! How did we cope?) The good thing about this time was that it gave young people the chance to get to know and understand each other in less pressurized environments, where they didn't need to worry about their every word or photo being shared. At that time, everything you said to each other had to be face to face or over the phone. This slowed down a relationship, because often the things you may be tempted to say in a text, you'd never dare to say out loud!

It went a bit like this: a girl would meet a boy (or a girl would meet a girl, or a boy would meet a boy) and they would start "going out". They would get to know each other well, and they would care about what the other person thought about them. They might hold hands, steal a sneaky kiss, or talk for ages over the phone. And, even though today it might seem scary or odd to talk over the phone, talking out loud to one another is still a much better way to get to know someone than just messaging. This is largely because it can be hard to work out the meaning of a text message. It's often very easy to misconstrue a written message because you can't hear how someone is saying it.

Rather than FaceTiming or messaging, couples would have to go out together on dates; they might go to the cinema, to the park, or to each other's houses. They didn't have the option of sexting or sending nude pictures. Instead they had to spend intimate time together to see one another like that. The fact they had to meet up to see each other meant they got to feel closer to the other person and got their full attention. After all, we all know that when we text, we're often distracted by other things going on around us at the same time.

On top of all that, there didn't used to be such a big fear of humiliation or fear of having your private moments published for everyone to see. Sexual moments took place between just the two people in the relationship.

All these things reduced pressure on young people and allowed them to make mistakes without being humiliated by them.

Today, it can be hard to know the difference between real affection and "phone affection". What I mean by that is, it's so easy to quickly type an "I love you too" message when you don't really feel that inside, just to make the other person happy. If you say something to someone's face, it's often harder to hide your real feelings.

Because most of the contact you're likely to have with a boyfriend or girlfriend now will probably be online or through a screen, it can be so easy for things to get out of hand. Misinterpreting what your partner sends to you in a message, for example, might cause an unnecessary argument. A partner asking you to send a nude picture or have a sexual chat with them might lead you to feel very uncomfortable, and fearful of what they might do if you don't go along with it.

I want you to remember that whatever your relationship is like, mutual respect between you is a must. I also want you to remember that when you fancy someone, you should try to take the time to get to know them. What are they really like, and do they really like you, or could they be using you?

It's true that most boys think differently about relationships than girls do. Boys tend to be more focused on having sex, as they're driven by the hormone testosterone. Girls, when they are attracted to a boy, are more likely to desire love and romance. They are normally looking for affection and closeness, which, down the line, may lead to a sexual relationship, while boys will often want to have sex as soon as possible. It tends to be the case that boys aren't as emotional about sex.

I'm not saying boys don't fall in love – of course they do. I'm saying that, for the most part, boys can have sex without the need to be in love, or even care that much about the girl they are having sex with. I'm not saying this to excuse boys behaving badly – I'm trying to explain that there are sometimes differences between the sexes.

However, I want you to know that whether or not a person wants to have sex with you in a relationship, you should always make sure that both of you are ready for it to happen. If a person respects you, they'll understand if you don't want to be intimate with them until you feel comfortable with it. If someone is pushing you to do something too soon, or to do something you are not comfortable with, you should not be with them!

Remember that kindness, respect and consent for anything sexual is a must. You should never feel forced to do anything in a relationship (sexually or otherwise) you don't want to do.

BEING IN LOVE SHOULD FEEL GOOD!

Flirting is all part of school and growing up; to some extent, it teaches us how to interact with each other. Banter of this sort, when it's not done to hurt or humiliate, can be fun. Everyone gives as good as they get, and no one is harmed. But any behaviour that leaves you feeling bad about yourself, inferior to a partner, or emotionally or physically hurt is wrong.

Your feelings are important, and you always have the right to protect yourself from any harm of any kind.

I want you to make good decisions about who you let into your life and who you have a romantic relationship with. I want you to come through and out of your teenage years as a strong, wise and confident person.

To achieve this, you will need to know what a good relationship is, as well as how to spot a bad one. Below is a list of things you can look out for.

If you have a partner, do they ever:

- Get angry when you don't drop everything for them?
- Criticize the way you look or dress?
- Stop you from seeing friends or from talking to any other boys/girls?
- Want you to give up something you love doing, like a sport or out-of-school activity?
- Threaten you, or call you nasty things?
- Hit you, or look like they are going to hit you?
- Try to force you to go further sexually than you want to?
- Frighten you?

If you can answer "yes" to any one of these things, you're not in a good relationship – dump them!

Here are some signs that you are in a good relationship:

- They give you space to see your friends and do any activities you enjoy doing.

- They trust you and you trust them.

- They cheer you up when you're feeling low and go out of their way to make you happy.

- You can talk about anything together.

- They never force you to go further sexually than you want to.

- They respect you and make you feel good about yourself.

- They share your dreams and support you.

- They are proud of you when you do well at school and never envy your success.

Love as a teenager, whether you're a boy or a girl, is about attraction and closeness. It's about sharing the thoughts and feelings that we don't share with anyone else. You should feel supported, understood, cared about and accepted for who you are, in all the relationships you have. As I've said, you might not be in these relationships long term (because you're still growing as a person), but as you grow older and find someone who shares all your values, then long-term commitment will become important. Still, right now, attraction, closeness and respect are a great and healthy start, and whether your relationship lasts a few weeks or a few months, you're learning how to love and be loved in return – and that's pretty awesome!

And, it should be said, if you haven't had a relationship yet, don't panic – there's still so much time. It's always better to wait for the right person to come along than to rush into something with the wrong person!

OVERSHARING

Whether we're in a relationship or not, the phenomenon of sexting is something that the majority of young people will encounter at some point in their teenage years. Within sexting, the practice of "sending nudes" (i.e. exchanging nude or explicit photographs) is commonplace.

Firstly, it's important to say that it is illegal for children (i.e. under eighteens) in the UK to create this kind of content, as well as to transmit it to others. It is also illegal for others to possess, download, store or view this content. This is the case in Australia and across most of the US too.

The reason for it being illegal is that explicit content of young people counts as child exploitation – even if you are sending the picture to someone your own age and you don't feel exploited. Sending this kind of picture also exposes you to humiliation and blackmail, which is harmful to both your mental and physical health.

Despite all this, a study by the UK charities Childline and the NSPCC reported that six out of ten teenagers have been asked for sexual pictures or videos. What's even more shocking is that 40 per cent of the teens they spoke to had created the content they were asked for, and had sent it on to either a partner, a peer or – in 15 per cent of the cases – a total stranger!

But why would you send this kind of thing to someone you don't even know? If a total stranger asked you to strip off in the middle of the street as you were walking to school, would you? No, you wouldn't.

Perhaps because sending a nude photo appears to just be a part of today's culture, and because everyone seems to be doing it, you might be thinking: "Well, what's the big deal?" Perhaps you even consider it empowering, because you get to be in control of the image someone is seeing of you, and because you know you are sexually attractive to someone.

Unfortunately, sending a nude picture is never empowering for any young person, because it has the potential to turn sex into a threat. It takes the fun out of a relationship and replaces it with fear: the fear of being humiliated by your intimate photos being shared. No matter how charming a person may be when they ask you to send them explicit content, or how bad they try to make you feel for not doing what they ask you to, it is important that you realize the risk you are opening yourself up to by sending nudes. If a person cares about you, they will never pressure you into doing something you don't feel comfortable doing.

You were not put on this planet to be bullied into doing whatever other people ask of you. You have a mind of your own and you are equal to everyone else.

Be empowered and say no to the things you don't want to do.

As girls, we should not be ashamed of fancying other people and wanting to be fancied. We should not be ashamed of our sexuality. However, what you choose to do with some should be personal and private.

Having a partner should make you happy. It should be fun, and it should never bring fear, worry or misery into your life.

My simple advice is to never do anything on social media you would not want everyone you know to read or see.

Don't allow anyone to take pictures or videos of you naked, and don't send anyone a picture or video of you naked – even on platforms that promise to dissolve or erase the message in the seconds or minutes after it is viewed. We all know it only takes a second to take a screenshot, and then it exists forever – and can be sent and shared with anyone and everyone!

My advice is: don't take the risk.

If you need help getting pictures removed from online platforms, or if you are worried about a sext which is being used to blackmail you, talk to someone. I don't want you to be one of those young people who become so sad and anxious that they hurt themselves or think about taking their own life over sending a nude picture.

If you're being pressured into sending nude pictures, you might want to download the app Zipit. It was set up by the UK charity NSPCC, and it helps you to deal with and respond to unwanted requests from people online. It's very clever!

We all make mistakes in life. You are still young, and you can't be expected to solve all your problems alone. Please, never be afraid to ask for help.

GROOMING

As a young woman, your heart might be vulnerable, and sadly some people who realize this can take advantage of it in the worst possible way. Grooming doesn't have to be online; it can happen anywhere – even when you're hanging out with your friends in town on a bright, sunny day.

Girls, most of us want to meet someone who really cares about us as much as we do about them. I don't think any girl would say they want a partner who will use, hurt and abuse them. But the sad truth is that even though some guys may seem perfect, they may not be in reality.

Groomers are very clever and dangerous people. They're able to make you believe they love and care for you when in fact they don't. Their reason for being nice is because they want to use you and, in some cases, make money out of you. Most of the time groomers will be men, but please be aware that women can be groomers too. That sounds really scary, I know. I'm talking about this because I want you to know how to spot the signs of grooming and manipulation and keep yourself safe.

Cases of young girls being groomed by gangs of men are common in towns and cities across the UK. In America, this kind of child sexual exploitation is called "sex trafficking". The charity UNICEF has estimated that 300,000 children are abused like this every year in the US. Sadly, grooming and trafficking take place in the rest of the world too.

Put simply, grooming is the abuse of girls and boys, most often by older men who will appear to be sophisticated, funny, kind and nice – so that they easily win your trust.

Groomers can often seem so charming that it's easy for you to think you're dating "Mr Wonderful". After all, when someone is buying you nice things, saying sweet things to you and taking you to lovely places, it might be difficult to think they could be a bad person (or that they could have an ulterior motive for being so nice to you). It might also be very flattering to have a handsome older man, or a "cool" older girl, take an interest in you.

Groomers can strike anywhere – you might be hanging out with your friends, at a shopping centre, at the park, at a coffee shop or just walking down the street. Put simply, it could happen anywhere where they're able to strike up casual conversation. They will likely start by chatting and making you laugh. You'll like them – they'll make sure you do. It's a situation that's so easy to fall into. One minute they're saying hi, the next they know your name, where you live and your phone number.

Never give out your address or phone number in these circumstances. Better still, don't strike up a conversation with strangers in the first place. Don't fall for their flattery. If they're older than you it should send alarm bells ringing, because no older man should ever want to go out with a schoolgirl.

Groomers use all sorts of tricks to get you to trust and fall in love with them. A common tactic is for them to ask you lots of questions about you and your family. They're not interested in hearing the details of your life because they care about you – they just want to make you *feel* they care. By asking lots of questions, they are also building up a picture of your life which they can use to manipulate you and blackmail you with in the future.

At first, these men will likely make you feel cherished, cared for and grown up. They will treat you like a woman. These are all tricks the groomers use to get young girls to trust them – and it often works. After all, it's instilled in us from a young age to want to be swept off our feet by a man and bought nice things.

As teenage girls we often want to be treated as grown-ups, because we feel more grown up than we are. Our bodies are changing; we're attracted to other people and they're attracted to us. What we're not prepared for is to be manipulated. When we're young, we're automatically trusting. It's not your fault for being sucked in – it's the groomer's manipulative nature that's to blame.

Unfortunately, as soon as the groomer has fully earned your trust, everything changes: suddenly, he wants something in return. Usually a groomer will want sex, which girls, who think they're loved and are in a real relationship, are often happy to go along with (even if they're under the legal age to have sex). To a girl who has no experience of the grim realities of life, this is a truly cruel form of abuse.

The groomer may have alienated you from your family, so you may feel you can't go to them for help. This can leave you feeling alone and helpless to stop the abuse. This is a very familiar pattern. It can be the start of a cycle of abuse that can be hard to escape from, and you may think no one can help you. Please remember that there is always help out there. My hope, however, is that if you know what to look out for in the first place you will never need to get this help.

If you do find yourself in this type of situation, you must tell a trusted adult, your parents and the police.

I'm not writing about this to frighten you; I'm writing about this because I want you to know that people like this exist. I want you to know how to keep yourself safe and how to spot if you or a friend are being groomed. I want you to know this information because knowledge is power. In these cases, it's the power to protect yourself from harm.

You may think this could never happen to you – and I hope it won't – but sadly it could happen to anyone. It doesn't matter what your background is. You may have a very happy family life; you may not. You may be wealthy; you may not have much money. None of that matters, because whoever you are, you can still fall into the hands of these people. If you're not aware of these telltale signs, you could be lured into a dark and miserable world, and I don't want that for you.

I want you to see the best in people and know a good and healthy relationship when you see it, but I also want you to be able to spot the worst and be able to keep yourself safe.

THINGS TO REMEMBER

Use these pages to write down all the things you think are most important for you to remember from this chapter. Return to these pages every now and then, to remind yourself of all the things you should know to keep yourself safe and happy.

LIFE IS
TOUGH
BUT SO
ARE YOU

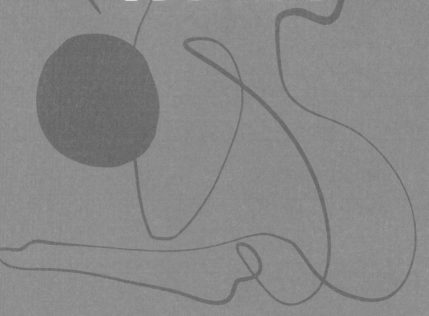

CHAPTER SEVEN

PORN IS NOT THE NORM

A lack of detailed sex education and relationship advice in schools (and perhaps also at home) means that your generation has got it pretty tough when it comes to working out what sex is really all about.

There's so much out there to misinform you about what sex is, and online pornography plays a particularly big part in spreading this misinformation. Worryingly, different surveys conducted right across the world show that watching online pornography is considered normal by many teenagers.

It's important you know that it's illegal to watch pornography if you're under 18. Porn is meant for adults and it is also fantasy; it was not made as a tool to teach young people about sex. Porn often puts both girls and boys at a big disadvantage when trying to understand what's normal in sexual encounters. Often, porn shows a very macho and one-sided view of sex.

In a survey by the UK children's charity the NSPCC, one 13-year-old girl who had watched porn said: "Consent is not shown... the man just does as he pleases."

Porn does not teach boys or girls how to have a relationship, or what love, consent and respect are; instead, most porn suggests that girls are little more than sexual objects, and it disempowers them in sexual encounters. The sort of sex you see in some porn videos can also be violent or extreme. It is not the "norm" for most people, or what many people would want to do.

But despite the dangers of porn – and the fact it is illegal for them to do so – most young people have seen or regularly watch pornography.

According to an NSPCC survey of more than 1,000 young people aged 11–16 in 2017:

- 48 per cent of 11–16-year-olds had seen pornography online.

- 28 per cent of 11–12-year-olds reported having seen pornography, though none of the girls claimed they had actively searched for it.

- More boys have watched online pornography than girls.

- 44 per cent of boys said that pornography had given them ideas about the types of sex they wanted to try compared to 29 per cent of girls.

In the course of the survey, one boy (aged 13) said: "One of my friends has started treating women like he sees in the videos – not major – just a slap here or there." This is scary!

A girl who was questioned in this survey (aged 13) said: "Well, you see what is happening in porn and you almost get worried about other people's relationships and it puts me off having any future relationships as it is very male dominated and not romantic or trusting."

Comments like these show us how easy it is for us to get very strange ideas about what sex should be like if we are learning from online pornography. And, while it's perfectly healthy and normal to be curious about sex, we should be mindful of where and what we are learning from.

It is worrying that the NSPCC also reports that girls who have sex at a young age are at risk of suffering from low self-esteem and possibly developing mental health issues.

Sex should not mess your head up, and it's certainly not something you have to rush to do. You should only have sex when you feel ready, and when you understand the facts.

SEX EDUCATION

Before I go any further, I want to make it clear that the legal age to have sex in the UK is 16. Across the world the legal age of consent varies from 11 years old (which seems like a worryingly young age!) to 21 years old. If you have sex before the legal age (or have sex with someone below the legal age) then you are breaking the law. This can have serious consequences for both you and your partner.

I am sure that some of you reading this won't feel ready to have sex at the legal age, and that is absolutely fine; everyone is different. What I want you to know more than anything is that having sex should be your decision – and no one else's!

So, let's just summarize a few things you should remember when it comes to sex:

ONE You don't have to have sex just because your friends are doing it, or because you feel pressured into it.

TWO Sex is not something you have to do to make boys like you.

THREE Sex should be just as pleasurable for a woman as it is for a man.

FOUR Sex is not a service you are here to provide to the world.

FIVE Sex is a mutual desire, and it is something that you should want to do just as much as your partner does.

SIX If you are forced to have sex, it is rape. This is a serious crime and one that must be reported to the police.

According to reports, abusive relationships between teenagers are on the rise. It goes without saying that this isn't healthy. Relationships are not meant to be like this at any stage of life.

Even though these statistics may not be directly related to the rise in young people watching porn, the ability to see sex portrayed in a controlling, emotionless – or sometimes even violent – way surely can't help.

Sex with someone you like and care about (and who cares about you) should never make you feel bad about yourself. It should be a wonderful, fun experience, and one that should make you feel good.

I am passionate that you understand that you have a right to an equal relationship – whether it's in sex or anything else!

Be sensible, be safe and be happy in whatever you choose.

The back of the book will give you some useful websites and resources that will help to answer all your questions about sex, as well as provide you with honest and reliable advice.

THINGS TO REMEMBER

Use this page to write down all the things you think are most important to remember in this chapter. Revisit this page whenever you need advice on how to be safe and sensible online.

IT'S NEVER TOO LATE TO LOOK AFTER YOURSELF

CHAPTER EIGHT

ANTI-SOCIAL MEDIA

It's pretty likely that most of you reading this are addicted to the many forms of social media there are out there, such as Instagram, Houseparty, Snapchat, Kik, Twitter, Holla, Facebook and WhatsApp. Undeniably, apps like these form a huge part of our lives. Sadly though, our reliance on them and our constant scrolling can turn social into anti-social media. We can easily become obsessed by them; in fact, scientists have found that in the UK a third of teenagers spend at least three hours a day on social media – with a fifth of teenagers spending at least five hours on it. In the US this shoots up to a shocking average of 7 hours and 22 minutes!

One thing that researchers from a variety of countries found is that those who were on social media for three hours or more a day were much more likely to get less sleep than those who were not glued to their phones. Researchers also showed that a lack of sleep put teenagers at risk of poorer results at school, and left young people open to mental health problems – as well as obesity, through lack of exercise.

I'm certainly not saying don't use social media; I'd be a hypocrite if I said this, because I use it myself. Not only do I use it, but I actually enjoy it – and it's great for my work as a journalist!

Social media has become a part of our culture, and most of you reading this will have never known life without it. It can be fun; it can make us laugh; it can keep us connected with family and friends we don't often see in real life. Social media can link us to new people, and those who share our interests; it can be a window on to worlds we couldn't easily see otherwise. It can even give you a creative outlet for your interests, such as vlogging. These things are clearly all good.

However, it's when it starts to make you feel bad about yourself – or perhaps even tearful or anxious – that alarm bells should be going off in your head. Not only can your relationship with social media become obsessive, but it can take you out of the real world. While we're scrolling for hours, we're not connecting face to face with people, and we miss out on going out into the world and doing things. Even simple things like going to the cinema, seeing people face to face and playing sport are critical to our well-being, and if we don't do them, we can be left feeling isolated.

Even though social media makes it seem like you're connected to people at all times, ultimately scrolling is a solitary pastime.

CYBERBULLYING

Social media creates a space that's a little bit unreal, and where we sometimes feel very safe, which can lead to us sharing far more than we should. Though it might seem like a good idea at the time, oversharing can leave you open to cyberbullies, trolls and haters, whose unkindness might really affect you.

At their worst, these comments can make people so sad they feel they no longer want to live. This breaks my heart. When you're young, these feelings can be even more intense and overwhelming because they take a grip on you that's hard to shake off. I don't ever want you to feel this way.

I'm not saying adults don't get affected in this way – they do – but they are generally more resilient due to their age and emotional experience.

Research in the *Journal of Medical Internet Research* has found that cyberbullying makes young people more than twice as likely to self-harm or attempt suicide. The research also found that teenagers and young people who were victims of cyberbullies were less likely to report it than people who were bullied physically or face to face.

Jesy Nelson, who shot to fame on *The X Factor* and is now part of the all-girl pop group Little Mix, has opened up about her own experience with trolling. Jesy has millions of fans, and like many in the public eye she uses social media. However, despite all the people who love and support her, she also has a lot of people criticizing her for how she looks and what she does. She has admitted that much of the online hate she received made her "want to die".

In a documentary she made on this topic, Jesy discussed the aftermath of her *X Factor* win – a time she should have felt on top of the world – and said the following:

"I had about 101 Facebook messages in my inbox, and the first one that came up was from some random man, saying: 'You are the ugliest thing I've seen in my life, you do not deserve to be in this girl band.'"

Jesy described how she didn't know how to deal with all of the online hate, and attempted suicide. She admitted that she was so low, she wasn't even thinking about what she was going to leave behind. Jesy advises young girls not to be so obsessed with social media, and to talk more to friends and family. Her personal story is something we could all learn from, as it shows you how incredibly damaging the words and actions of bullies can be – even to those people who look like they have the "perfect life".

So, how can you protect yourself and make yourself more resilient to this sort of thing?

Here are a few ideas:

ONE

CAPTURE EVIDENCE: screenshot the things bullies say to you, so that you have evidence when you tell someone about it.

TWO

BLOCK THEM: what you don't see or read can't harm you. I've blocked people who've sent me offensive material and it's done the trick.

THREE

REPORT IT: always report foul or offensive behaviour to the social media company you're using. Most social media companies have guidelines on how you can do this. You may need to get an adult to help you with this.

FOUR

TELL SOMEONE: find someone to confide in, whether it's a friend, parent, trusted adult or teacher. You could also call telephone helplines.

Cyberbullies can be very threatening. Their aim is to hurt, intimidate or humiliate you. Don't let them!

A preventative measure you can take against cyberbullying is to keep your accounts locked down to everyone except your real friends. Of course, some of the people that troll or cyberbully can turn out to be people you know, but this should help prevent it from happening. Also, before you post anything, ask yourself: "If the whole world saw this post – my mum and dad and teachers included – how would I feel?" If you feel OK about that, then go ahead and post. If you feel anxious, maybe think again!

TELL SOMEONE

If you are being bullied, getting help is vital; tell someone you trust about it. I cannot overstate the importance of this. A problem is never such a big problem if you share it.

Talk to a friend, parent, teacher or anyone who is looking after you. Trust me, you will feel a big sense of relief once you know you're not facing the problem alone. It might be hard to talk about what people are saying about you, or it might be embarrassing to tell someone what you posted that started it all – but it'll be so worth it. Even if you can't bring yourself to do it face to face, write it down and hand the note to them.

Nothing is ever worth so much worry that it makes you unhappy or – worse – makes you feel like you want to harm yourself.

I'm not saying it will always be easy to talk about cyberbullying, but in the end, it will be for the best, and you will feel OK again. You just have to trust me on this: don't try to deal with it on your own. If you have no one to talk to or feel you'd rather talk to a stranger, you can call one of the many hotlines run by children's charities. You'll find details for some of these at the back of the book.

DON'T COMPARE YOURSELF(IE)

Let's face it: most of the stuff posted on social media is a bit "meh". Pictures of people's food, endless selfies... Enough said.

When we post stuff online, we often do it because we want others to see the best version of ourselves. We want to look awesome!

When we scroll along our feeds, there are usually endless photos of people looking super cool and utterly beautiful. When all we see is "perfect" people having the time of their lives, it's no surprise that we're left feeling lonely, sad and dissatisfied with our looks and our social lives.

COMPARISON IS THE THIEF OF JOY

This feeling of dissatisfaction used to come mainly from glossy magazines, with famous people staring out at us and looking perfect (thanks to airbrushing!). Nowadays, the technology available means we can all look "perfect". We can all remove our (perceived) imperfections, make ourselves thinner, have bigger eyes and flawless skin – the changes are endless! But these "imperfections" are something we all have, and they work together to form who we are.

When I look online, it's so easy to find articles telling me what the best apps are for flawless selfies – but, by using these apps, what we are actually saying to the world is that we are not good enough as we are. This mindset is not only very sad, but also dangerous when it comes to how we view ourselves. We start to worry needlessly, and obsess about how we look, and in the long run, we can do serious damage to our self-esteem, and that can make us dislike ourselves. It can stop us finding our inner sparkle and being successful and happy.

People of all genders have always been judged for their appearance, but girls and women tend to be judged much more than men and boys. For a long time, women have fought hard not to be judged on their looks, but rather for what they can do or what they have achieved. By using these "perfecting" apps, we are going backward and allowing society to dictate that, no matter what we achieve, the way we look is the most important thing about us.

Flinders University in Australia carried out some research on this topic, involving more than 1,000 schoolgirls. The study found that teenage conversations about appearance were "intensified" on social media and were more influential than traditional media because comments from peers were seen to be of the utmost importance.

Experts from the university found that time spent on social networking sites was linked to lower self-esteem, lower body confidence, lack of identity and higher depression rates.

It's not just how we look though – it's also about what we see people doing on social media that can make us feel sad. Pictures of people leading what look like brilliantly exciting lives can make us feel lonely too. We can end up worrying that we are not popular enough, or that we are leading boring lives compared to our friends.

The UK children's charity Childline says a growing number of teenagers is contacting them about being lonely. In fact, in 2017–2018, Childline carried out nearly 5,000 sessions to help children with feelings of loneliness. Girls received almost 80 per cent of these sessions, primarily raising concerns about the harmful effects of social media and how comparing themselves to others online made them feel increasingly isolated.

It is therefore very important that you try not to compare your life to the lives you see on social media. The truth is: no one's life is exciting all the time – that's just not how life works!

SURVIVING SOCIAL!

As I mentioned before, social media can educate us and help us make links with things we're interested in – but it can also badly misinform. There are so many websites that are disreputable, and which are giving out false or dangerous information. In particular, sites that encourage girls to obsess about their weight and their looks are common. But there are even sites out there that encourage people to self-harm or to hurt others. We all have to be very careful about what we look at online and what we learn from social media.

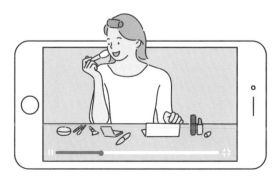

SOMETIMES THE GRASS IS GREENER

BECAUSE IT'S FAKE

Of course, free speech is great, but it does not mean that anyone should go online and give out their personal views on any issue. The fact that people do do this means that we should always be aware that what we're reading could be someone's opinion, and not fact.

Use social media to follow organizations and people who make a difference – a good difference! Any site or person who is preaching fear, hate or is encouraging you to feel unhappy with yourself should be avoided.

Once you've curated your social media to be a more positive place for you to spend your time, consider cutting down the amount of time you spend on it. Try, for instance, not to take your phone to bed. Just switch it off a little while before you go to bed and focus on a good night's sleep. Not only will doing this help improve the quality of your sleep, but it'll also feel surprisingly liberating!

Energy and drive are so important in this life; these are among the things we need to be ambitious, to succeed and to be awesome.

So, learn from the lessons in this chapter, apply them to your life, and you'll have a safe and positive relationship with social media in no time.

MY RELATIONSHIP WITH SOCIAL MEDIA

Use this page to write down all the things you think are most important to remember in this chapter. Revisit this page whenever you need advice on how to be safe and sensible online.

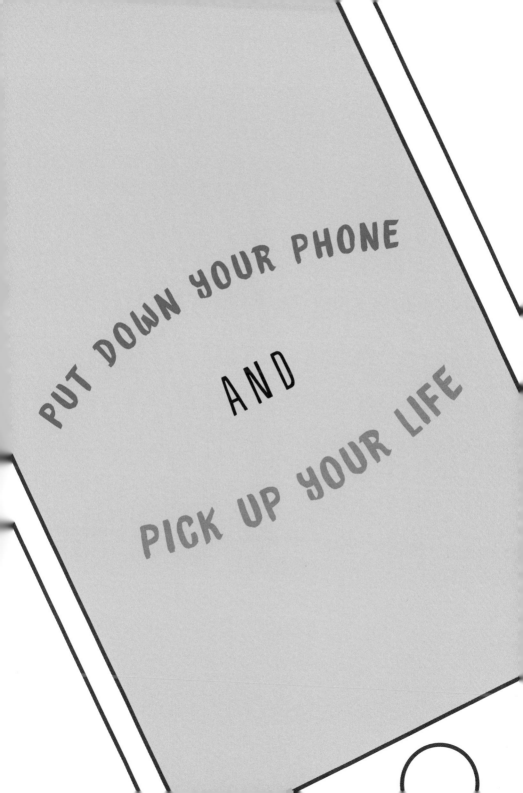

CHAPTER NINE

THE "F" WORD: FEMINISM

> **"SO, IF I DON'T HAVE SEX WITH YOU, I'M A PRUDE; IF I USE THE PILL, I'M A SLUT; IF I GET PREGNANT, I'M AN IDIOT; IF I EVER HAVE AN ABORTION, I'M THE DEVIL."**

This anonymous quote stands out to me as an excellent example of why we still need feminism. This quote really calls out the double standards women face when it comes to sex, as they go right from teenagerhood to their adult years. Ironically, men often seem to be immune from these sorts of cruel insults and prejudices. Perhaps society has forgotten that it takes two people to have sex (and to make a baby)!

EQUALITY OR SUPERIORITY?

Sadly, feminism is an uncomfortable word for some. Even the feminist Sheryl Sandberg has acknowledged the difficulty that some women face in identifying with the movement:

> **"I'M A FEMINIST BECAUSE I BELIEVE IN WOMEN... IT'S A HEAVY WORD, FEMINISM, BUT IT'S NOT ONE I THINK WE SHOULD RUN FROM. I'M PROUD TO BE A FEMINIST."**
>
> **SHERYL SANDBERG, CHIEF OPERATING OFFICER OF FACEBOOK, AUTHOR AND PHILANTHROPIST**

Some people still hold the outdated view that all feminists are angry and man-hating. Bizarrely, it's also sometimes assumed that if you're a feminist, you're also a lesbian. Well, the truth is, whether you're a lesbian, a heterosexual or anything outside of this, you can still be a feminist. Perhaps it would even surprise you to know that men can be feminists too – and many are!

To me, it's very odd that any girl wouldn't be a feminist. After all, this is like saying: "I don't value my rights, and I agree that men are superior to me." I hope that by now (having read most of this book) you know these assumptions are totally wrong. However, there are people in the world who do think like this, and that's exactly why we need feminism.

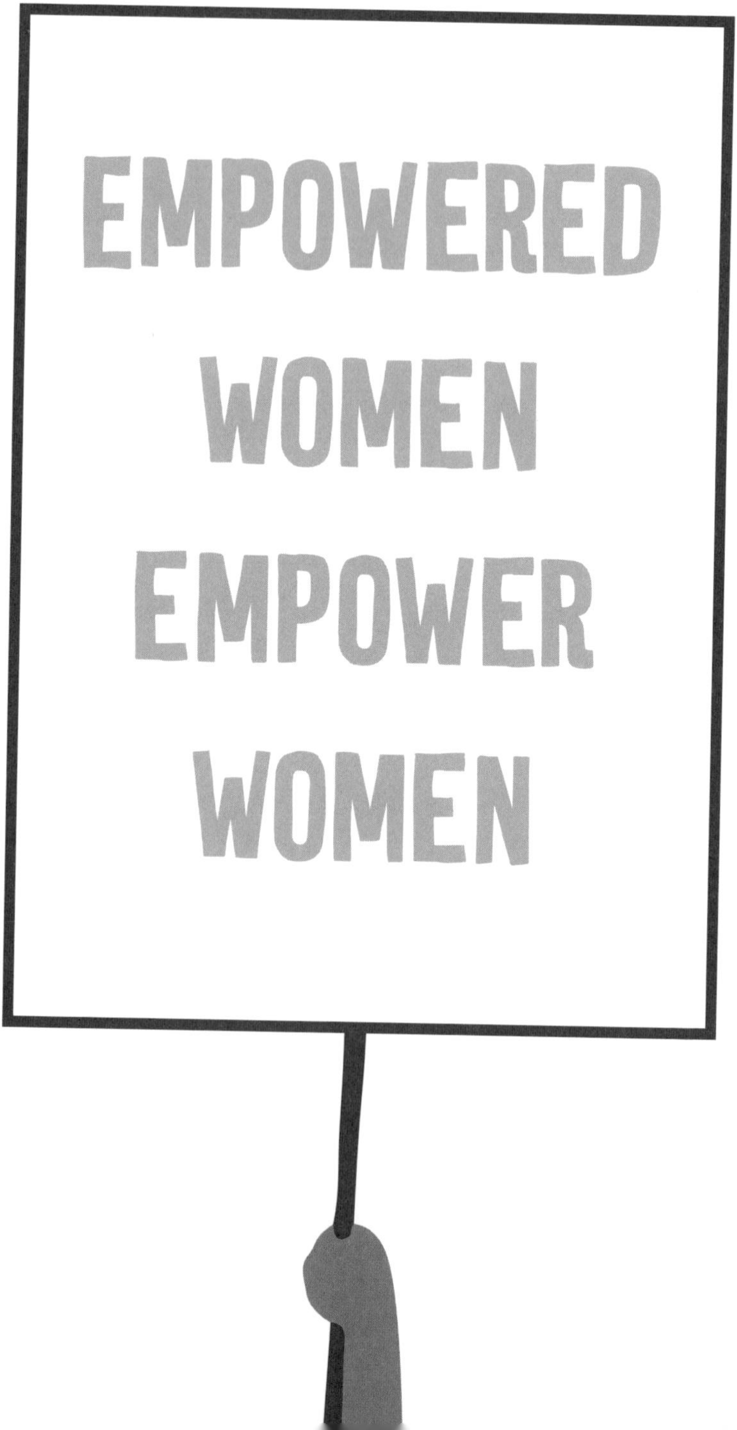
EMPOWERED
WOMEN
EMPOWER
WOMEN

> "I MYSELF HAVE NEVER BEEN ABLE TO FIND OUT PRECISELY WHAT
> FEMINISM IS: I ONLY KNOW THAT PEOPLE CALL ME FEMINIST WHEN I
> EXPRESS SENTIMENTS THAT DIFFERENTIATE ME FROM A DOORMAT."

REBECCA WEST, BRITISH AUTHOR AND JOURNALIST

Perhaps so many women struggle to embrace feminism because it sounds too tough. Some women hate the word so much that, although they believe in the principles of feminism, they won't actually call themselves a feminist – simply because the word itself carries so much prejudice.

Amazingly, fewer than one in five young women would call themselves a feminist according to polling in the US and the UK. Judging by this statistic, it seems that we need to take the fear out of feminism.

As far as I'm concerned, feminism isn't just a word that belongs to women – it belongs to everyone who agrees that women are equal to men. Among other things, feminism advocates that women should be treated fairly, and that they should have the same opportunities as men. I don't see what's wrong with those things – do you?

Being a feminist doesn't mean you want to punish men, or that you don't like them. It doesn't mean that you don't appreciate it when a man offers to help you, or when he holds a door open for you. After all, when a man helps you, it doesn't mean you can't do something for yourself – of course you can – it often just means they're being kind or polite. This is the same thing as if a woman offered to help a man or held a door open for him! Women are not looking for special treatment – just equal treatment.

Feminism also means acknowledging that your viewpoint on issues is just as important and valid as anyone else's, of any gender.

FIGHTING FOR FEMINISM

Over 100 years ago in the UK, a militant women's organization called the suffragettes fought for women's rights. Some of these women were jailed – and some even died – in the fight for women to be given the vote. This happened in other countries across the world too.

Although voting seems like a basic human right to many of us now, it used to be something that only men were allowed to do (and in some countries voting rights are still very limited for women). Back when women in the UK were not allowed to vote, it was widely believed by most men (and even some women) that if women were allowed to vote, women would:

- Be corrupted by politics.

- Stop getting married and having children.

- Be too emotional, and therefore incapable of making good political decisions.

For anyone to say any of this to a woman nowadays would be laughable. After all, we have seen now how incredibly effective and successful women in politics can be!

The suffragettes were most definitely feminists. They proved that you can change things for the better if you're prepared to speak up rather than suffer in silence.

MY FEMINIST ICONS

Use this page to write down all the amazing feminists in your own life. Think about all the women you look up to, and how each of them supports the females around them.

DO WE STILL NEED FEMINISM?

Today, many people say we don't need feminism any more; these people point to women around the world who have become politicians, or who lead their countries, or who fight alongside men in military conflicts. So really, how much more equality do women need?

The answer to that question is: a lot more. Whenever I hear, for instance, that some women and girls are missing work or school because they can't afford sanitary products, I am reminded of how much work there is still left to be done.

If you assumed that period poverty is only a problem in developing countries, you'd be mistaken. In the UK, it wasn't until January 2020 that the government committed to ensuring that free sanitary products would be provided to all those who need them – but for too many girls and women around the world, they are sadly not so lucky. Period poverty, for many women and girls, forces them to stay at home and that can mean either falling behind at school or losing money each month from their pay packet.

When I read a report that said 90 per cent of British women have reported being harassed in the street before the age of 17, I was once again reminded of how much we still need feminism. In the US, an equally shocking 85 per cent of women reported that they had suffered street harassment before they were 17.*

Catcalling, unwanted sexual touching, upskirting (which means taking pictures up girls' and women's skirts without their knowledge or consent) are all actions which leave women feeling humiliated, vulnerable and sometimes fearful – yet these are things that happen to women every day.

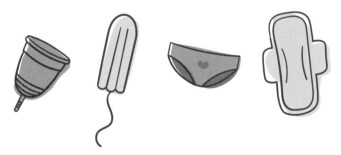

* Hollaback! and Cornell University (2015)

Although upskirting is now a criminal offence in the UK, there is not yet a specific law against street harassment. Interestingly, in the US, many forms of street harassment are illegal – and that's the case in France too.

Sadly, this is happening to women and girls of all ages.

According to the charity Plan International UK, one in three girls in the UK has received unwanted sexual attention and one in seven has been followed while in their school uniform.

Of course, there will always be people who tell you to "get over it" if anything like this has happened to you – or who tell you "it's just banter" and that "you should be flattered". But just remember that anything that's done without your consent – or that makes you feel scared or humiliated – is not OK.

We still need feminism so that people understand that no one has the right to make sexually explicit comments toward others, based on their gender, their looks, or what they're wearing. No one has the right to touch or harass others, whatever the context.

Another big reason that I believe we still need feminism is to stop the outrageous practice of "victim-blaming". This is, essentially, where the victim of a crime is held wholly (or partly) responsible for whatever has happened to them; sadly, this can (and does) happen to women who have been sexually assaulted or raped.

When people hear that a woman has been raped or sexually assaulted, they often also hear about what that woman was wearing, if she had been drinking, and if she was out late at night when the attack happened. These things are sometimes used as tools to determine whether or not the victim was to blame for the attack they suffered. They are used to provide some sort of explanation for why the attack happened, or to explain why it wasn't entirely the fault of the perpetrator. I hope you're as enraged by this as I am!

Although I'm not suggesting that getting drunk doesn't leave you vulnerable, the fact is that whether you're drunk or sober, fully dressed or hardly wearing anything, no sexual attack is ever your fault, nor is it excusable.

No woman asks to be sexually assaulted or raped. It is never the victim's fault. The attacker is the one committing the crime. It's not a crime to dress or look a certain way, and it's not a crime to trust someone, or to walk along a street at night. It is, however, a crime to rape someone.

I can't think of any other crime where the victim, rather than the offender, is blamed for it.

We still need feminism because this attitude needs to stop.

But, quite honestly, there are countless reasons we still need feminism. I have listed just a few more reasons below, for you to keep in mind:

ONE

Many women still don't get paid equally to men.

TWO

In many countries, girls are prevented from going to school.

THREE

Around 41,000 girls are forced into marriage every day around the world.

FOUR

The dangerous and painful practice of FGM (female genital mutilation – where girls have their genitals cut away to stop them having pleasurable sex and make sure they're faithful to their husbands) is still practised in around 29 countries across the world, despite campaigns to stop it. Around the world, more than 200 million girls and women are living in pain as a result.

FIVE

3.8 million women and girls across some African countries are suffering breast ironing. This is the pounding and flattening of young girls' breasts to protect them from unwanted male attention and sexual harassment.

SIX

Women in many countries are denied the right to contraception, and to decide if and when to have a baby.

All of these things keep women and girls unequal to men in society. As a woman, and as a proud feminist, I don't want special rights – I just want basic human rights, and fairness and equality for women everywhere in the world.

As Hillary Clinton, former US First Lady and politician, put it: "Human rights are women's rights and women's rights are human rights, once and for all."

The battle to get everyone to see this has not yet been won.

SHE NEEDED A HERO,

SO

THAT'S

WHAT

SHE

BECAME

CHAPTER TEN

GOODBYE AND GOOD LUCK

Everything I have talked about in this book is meant to make you feel empowered, informed and – most of all – awesome!

Right now, you should be tingling with excitement about your future. As young as you are, I hope that in some small way this book has set you on an exciting track toward becoming the woman you want to be, as well as helped you work out what you want from life and how you are going to get it.

Try not to dwell on the fact that the world is unfair. Just take every day one step at a time. Whenever you find that you're doubting yourself, or struggling to believe that you can ever achieve your dreams, look up the stories of the strong, successful women I have quoted in this book and the many other women out there who have overcome obstacles and gone on to great things. Or even just take a look at the inspirational women in your own life and talk to them about what they did to get where they are today.

Look up the struggles of the suffragettes and the other amazing women all over the world who fought so hard to achieve awesome things for us all to enjoy today.

It's incredible to think of women all those years ago being so passionate about getting equal rights that they were even prepared to die for the cause. It should inspire us all to know those women achieved those things – despite the hatred and anger shown toward them – so that our lives could be better today.There will be days when you feel the world is against you, and that nothing seems to go right; everyone has these days! But try not to let those moments get you down. Put on some music you love, read or watch something inspirational, or go and do something that makes you happy. Whatever it takes, get yourself back on track. Remember that worrying never improved a bad situation; the only thing that will help is having a plan to change it.

I hope that by now you are involved in some extracurricular activities which will help to stretch your mind and enable you to have new, positive experiences. I hope you're excited and driven about the sort of life you want to build. I hope you're excited about the relationships you have (or will have), and wise to the ones you should avoid.

The good things in this world exist for each and every one of us. Whether we are born rich or poor, we are all just flesh and blood; we all have potential.

I hope you know never to feel inferior to anyone. Remember "sparkle"? Your voice – and what you use it for – is just as important as anyone else's. I hope you also realize that you do not have to follow the crowd, but that you are your own person.

Life should be fun; you should be able to study hard and play hard. Be kind to yourself, be kind to others and treat everyone the way you want to be treated.

Really think about what you want from life and determine to go and get it. Be proud to be a strong, independent girl, and don't be frightened of hard work or standing out from the crowd. It will make you an awesome person.

Finally, I found this, and I wanted to share it with you.

"IF A CHILD LIVES WITH CRITICISM, SHE LEARNS TO CONDEMN.
IF A CHILD LIVES WITH HOSTILITY, SHE LEARNS TO FIGHT.
IF A CHILD LIVES WITH RIDICULE, SHE LEARNS TO BE SHY.
IF A CHILD LIVES WITH SHAME, SHE LEARNS TO FEEL GUILTY.
IF A CHILD LIVES WITH TOLERANCE, SHE LEARNS TO BE PATIENT.
IF A CHILD LIVES WITH ENCOURAGEMENT, SHE LEARNS CONFIDENCE.
IF A CHILD LIVES WITH PRAISE, SHE LEARNS TO APPRECIATE.
IF A CHILD LIVES WITH FAIRNESS, SHE LEARNS JUSTICE.
IF A CHILD LIVES WITH SECURITY, SHE LEARNS TO HAVE FAITH.
IF A CHILD LIVES WITH APPROVAL, SHE LEARNS TO LIKE HERSELF.
IF A CHILD LIVES WITH ACCEPTANCE AND FRIENDSHIP,
SHE LEARNS TO FIND LOVE IN THE WORLD."

ANONYMOUS

Always remember that you are awesome. Truly believe it; be different and dare to make your dreams come true.

WHAT HAVE I LEARNED?

Use these pages to note down some of the most important lessons you have learned from this book. Revisit these pages as often as you like, to keep the information fresh in your mind.

THIS IS THE BEGINNING

OF
ANYTHING
YOU WANT

RESOURCES

For further general information or advice:

UK:

CHILDLINE: www.childline.org.uk or call 0800 1111

TEEN ISSUES: www.teenissues.co.uk

HELP TO HEAL: www.helptoheal.co.uk or call 01708 765200

THE MIX: www.themix.org.uk or call 0808 808 4994

SUPPORTLINE: www.supportline.org.uk or call 01708 765 200

US:

CHILDHELP: www.childhelp.org

GIRL UP: www.girlup.org

GIRLS' HEALTH: www.girlshealth.gov

AUSTRALIA:

BEYOND BLUE: www.beyondblue.org.au or call 1300 22 4636

For further information or advice about gender identity:

UK:

THE BEAUMONT TRUST: www.beaumont-trust.org.uk or call 01582 412 220

US:

TRANS YOUTH EQUALITY FOUNDATION: www.transyouthequality.org

AUSTRALIA:

INTERSEX HUMAN RIGHTS AUSTRALIA: ihra.org.au

REACH OUT: www.au.reachout.com

For further information and advice about sex:

UK:

SEXWISE: www.sexwise.fpa.org.uk

BROOK: www.brook.org.uk

NHS SEXUAL HEALTH HELPLINE: 0300 123 7123

US:

AMERICAN SEXUAL HEALTH ASSOCIATION: www.ashasexualhealth.org

AUSTRALIA:

HEALTH DIRECT: www.healthdirect.gov.au/sexual-health

RELATIONSHIPS AUSTRALIA: www.relationships.org.au

FAMILY PLANNING: www.fpnsw.org.au

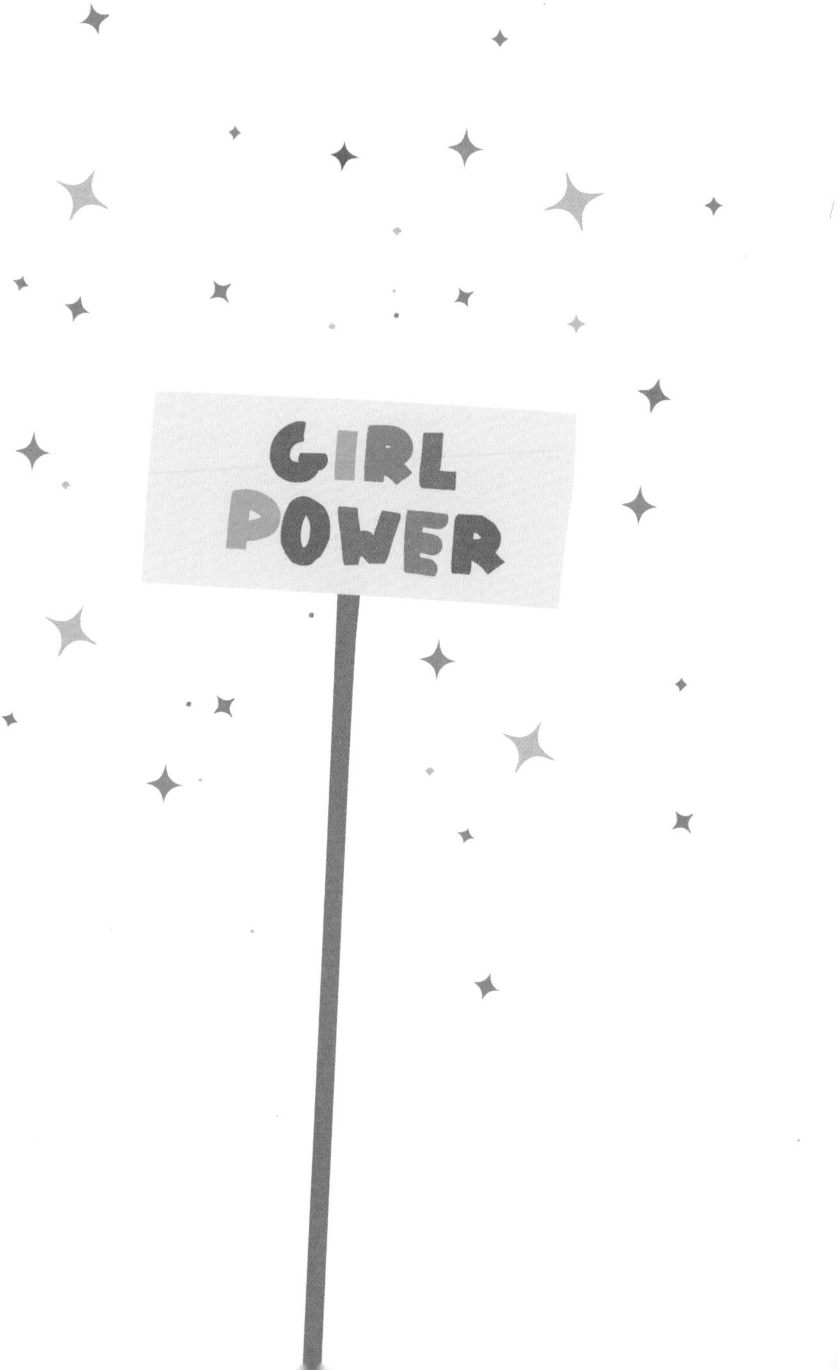
GIRL
POWER

IMAGE CREDITS

pp.1, 3, 9, 22, 40, 94 – highlighter © samui/Shutterstock.com; pp.4, 13, 14, 18, 23, 26–27, 28–29, 58–59, 60, 68, 70, 80–81, 152–153, 154–155, 158, 160 – stars © Vdant85/Shutterstock.com; pp.4, 6–7, 10–11, 58–59, 61, 62, 64, 68, 70–71, 72, 74, 80–81, 152–153 – stars outline © Astarina/Shutterstock.com; pp.9, 49 – hand © puxnd/Shutterstock.com; p.15 – people © Nadia Snopek/Shutterstock.com; p.16 – woman and ladder © MJgraphics/Shutterstock.com; p.19 – thought bubble © ONYXprj/Shutterstock.com; pp.20–21 – speech bubbles © ONYXprj/Shutterstock.com; p.24 – woman in bubble © venimo/Shutterstock.com; p.30 – hand © venimo/Shutterstock.com; p.33 – book © Singleline/Shutterstock.com; p.34 – flasks © Singleline/Shutterstock.com; p.35 – notebook © Singleline/Shutterstock.com; p.38 – tools © Singleline/Shutterstock.com; p.41 – space man © Singleline/Shutterstock.com; p.42 – girl with book © Singleline/Shutterstock.com; pp.45, 46–47, 49, 55 – light bulb © GoodStudio/Shutterstock.com; p.50 – rosette © Blan-k/Shutterstock.com; p.52 – car © Andre Adams/Shutterstock.com; p.53 – medal © PaintDoor/Shutterstock.com; pp.56–57 – hurdles © Olha Turchenko/Shutterstock.com; pp.61, 62, 75 – thumbs © Astarina/Shutterstock.com; pp.66–67 – hands © oxygen_8/Shutterstock.com; p.69 – hands and heart © Yourbookkeeper/Shutterstock.com; pp.72, 74, 79 – hands © puxnd/Shutterstock.com; p.76, 158 – girl with sign © Nicetoseeya/Shutterstock.com; p.78 – glasses © Nicetoseeya/Shutterstock.com; pp.79, 82–83, 85, 86, 91, 151 – shapes © Nicetoseeya/Shutterstock.com; p.87 – girl meditating © Nicetoseeya/Shutterstock.com; p.88 – girl on bike © Nicetoseeya/Shutterstock.com; p.90 – girl crossing arms © Nicetoseeya/Shutterstock.com; pp.92–93 – gender signs © cosmaa/Shutterstock.com; p.98 – girl with thought bubble © cosmaa/Shutterstock.com; p.99 – girls talking © cosmaa/Shutterstock.com; pp.101, 100, 107 – girl with hearts © cosmaa/Shutterstock.com; p.103 – woman holding heart © cosmaa/Shutterstock.com; pp.104–105 – people texting © cosmaa/Shutterstock.com; p.108 – phone in hand © cosmaa/Shutterstock.com; p.108 – pixels © milart/Shutterstock.com; p.109 – woman crying © cosmaa/Shutterstock.com; p.111 – woman with speech bubble © cosmaa/Shutterstock.com; p.110 – man fishing in phone © cosmaa/Shutterstock.com; p.112 – heart in bubble © cosmaa/Shutterstock.com; p.113 – speech bubble © cosmaa/Shutterstock.com; p.114 – hands giving heart © cosmaa/Shutterstock.com; pp.118, 119 120, 122 – line drawing © KNST ART STUDIO/Shutterstock.com; p.124 – moon and stars © KNST ART STUDIO/Shutterstock.com; p.126 – phone in hand © adehoidar/Shutterstock.com; pp.127, 129 – bubble with signs © Pranch/Shutterstock.com; pp.125, 128 – hand and phone © adehoidar/Shutterstock.com; p.137 – phone © autumn/Shutterstock.com; p.138 – flag © FishPouch/Shutterstock.com; pp.139, 146–147 – loudspeaker © Adrian Niederhaeuser/Shutterstock.com; p.141 – women standing together © Nicetoseeya/Shutterstock.com; p.142 – girls protesting © venimo/Shutterstock.com; p.144 – sanitary products © mamormo/Shutterstock.com; p.145 – posters © GoodStudio/Shutterstock.com; pp.130, 132–133, 135 – girl in phone © autumn/Shutterstock.com; p.151 – hands © oxygen_8/Shutterstock.com

Have you enjoyed this book?

If so, why not write a review on your favourite website?

If you're interested in finding out more about our books,

find us on Facebook at **Summersdale Publishers**

and follow us on Twitter at **@Summersdale**.

Thanks very much for buying this Summersdale book.

www.summersdale.com